TEMPORARY INSANITY

JAY JOHNSTONE

WITH RICK TALLEY

CONTEMPORARY
BOOKS, INC.
CHICAGO

Library of Congress Cataloging in Publication Data

Johnstone, Jay, 1946—
    Temporary insanity.

    1: Johnstone, Jay, 1946—   2. Baseball players—
United States—Biography.   3. Baseball—United States.
I. Talley, Rick.   II. Title.
GV865.J63A37   1985   796.357′092′4 [B]   85-12585
ISBN 0-8092-5191-4

To Mary Jayne, my first and only wife, and
Mary Jayne Sarah, my first and only child

Published by Contemporary Books, Inc.
180 North Michigan Avenue, Chicago, Illinois 60601
Manufactured in the United States of America
Library of Congress Catalog Card Number: 85-12585
International Standard Book Number: 0-8092-5191-4

Published simultaneously in Canada by Beaverbooks, Ltd.
195 Allstate Parkway, Valleywood Business Park
Markham, Ontario L3R 4T8 Canada

CONTENTS

IN GLOWING PRAISE OF JAY JOHNSTONE

I can't think of a ball player I'd rather have in a clubhouse than Jay Johnstone. But he wrote a book? What with, a fire extinguisher? Shaving cream?

Let me tell you what it's like to have Jay on a baseball team. It's like leaving your house to go fishing for four days. And just as you step into the boat, you remember that you left the back door of your house open. Now you don't know if somebody is back there stealing everything in your house, but you can't sleep for four days worrying about it.

That's how I feel about Johnstone. I never know what he's going to do, but I can't sleep for worrying about it. I just know that something is coming.

Some people are naturally funny, you know? But Jay is more than funny. He's crazy. There are a lot of people in asylums who are saner than Jay Johnstone. He's also devious. He must sit up nights, thinking of new things to do to me.

Like the time he stole all the pictures out of my office. I must have had 200 pictures—autographed pictures of people like Frank Sinatra and Don Rickles. So one day I come in from the field, and all the pictures are gone. All four walls are blank except for three pictures. There was an autographed picture of Jay Johnstone on one wall, one of Don Stanhouse on another, and one of Jerry Reuss on another.

But I love Jay. He's good for a team. I like humor in the clubhouse, and Jay has that wonderful knack for making other people laugh. I've screamed at him and fined him— but I've never really been mad at him. Not really. How can you get mad at somebody who keeps a baseball team so loose?

I will say this, though. He's the only player I've ever managed who needs a beeper. I can never find him. I can't imagine how he finds so many places to hide.

Then out of nowhere he'll show up where he's not supposed to be, like at my dinner table when he isn't invited. Somehow he always knows where I'm going for dinner. Once I made reservations for 12 people at a really nice restaurant—big, circular table, the whole works—and when I got there, Jay was already sitting at the table eating bread sticks. Another time I was speaking at one of those father-son dinners, out in San Gabriel or somewhere, and I look down in the front row and there sits Jay Johnstone, grinning. He never knew one guy in that room but somehow found out where I was speaking and came over just to sit there and stare at me.

How do you keep ahead of him? During spring training this year, for example, we were really working hard—well-organized, a lot of emphasis on fundamentals, a tight schedule, you know? Then one day one of our coaches looked at his clipboard and noticed that somebody had written on the schedule "11 to 11:15: Brake for Johnstone and Russell." Not only had he written it on three different schedules; he had misspelled *break* all three times.

But I'll tell you something else about Jay Johnstone. No ball player has ever worked harder to keep himself in shape and make himself a good hitter, which he became. He's tireless. And once he walks onto that field, nobody is more serious about winning.

It's just that Jay thinks differently from most of us. What's that saying about some people marching to the beat of a different drummer? Johnstone must hear a symphony out there. One night at Dodger Stadium I'm sitting there worrying about how the game is going, and I look up at Diamond Vision, our big TV screen, and the camera has caught Jay and Reuss wearing groundskeepers' uniforms, and they're out there dragging the infield. I was dumbfounded. One inning later he hits a home run. He has to be the only man in baseball history to drag the infield one inning and hit a home run the next. Got to be. But I'll let Jay give you the details in this book, *Temporary Insanity*.

That's some book title. But I'm not so sure about the temporary part.

Tom Lasorda, Manager
Los Angeles Dodgers

A HEARTFELT TRIBUTE TO MY TALLER FRIEND

I first met Jay Johnstone in Hermosillo, Mexico, during the Caribbean World Series of 1974. He was telling stories and laughing, orchestrating an evening that anyone would enjoy. I liked what I saw. This was a man getting some fun out of life.

Five years later, when Jay joined the Dodgers, our friendship began slowly. He gave me a chocolate hand by putting a brownie in my glove, then a stained head by putting chewing tobacco in my batting helmet. But somewhere along the way of running stadium steps, hitting thousands of baseballs, and doing everything we could to win, we became friends. We also had fun.

Jay shared his wit and friendship with me when it was most needed. I added a certain sane balance which he appreciated.

Jay will make a statement with this book—one which I hope will refresh your feelings about professional sports and those who play the games.

And I guarantee he will make you laugh.

Steve Garvey,
First Baseman
San Diego Padres

"

Consider the Penguin, Ron Cey. *The National League Green Book* lists him at 5'9", 185, but I believe he stands closer to 5'7", with his weight evenly distributed between his muscles and his teeth.

"

CHAPTER

1

PENGUINS
AND OTHER
COLD DUCKS

"Just once I'd like to slip up behind Johnstone and smash a cream pie in his face."

Al Campanis

Nothing is sacred in a baseball clubhouse.

You give and you take and nobody gets a pass. Not even the superstars.

Some ball players, of course, are easier targets than others. By their appearance and attitude, they ask for special attention, and there is almost always somebody like me, eager to oblige.

Consider the Penguin, Ron Cey. *The National League Green Book* lists him at 5'9", 185, but I believe he stands closer to 5'7", with his weight evenly distributed between his muscles and his teeth. And you only have to watch him run to his position at third base for the Chicago Cubs one time to understand the origin of the nickname. Sports columnist Jim Murray of the *Los Angeles Times* once asked about Ronnie: "Why do they call him the Penguin when he waddles like a duck?"

Penguin is also a wonderful target for clubhouse humor because of his demeanor. He has no personality (I call him

1

Mr. Charm), seldom smiles, and gets irritated about as quickly as anybody I've ever known. I own Pengy.

It was spring training 1980, when Ronnie and I both played with the Dodgers, that I gave him a new locker. That should prove right there that I like the guy. There aren't many teammates who would do what I did for the Penguin that morning in Dodgertown.

What I did was cut his locker down to Penguin size. I started at 7:00 A.M., and it took me about an hour and a half. But it was worth it.

First I got some wood just like that of Cey's locker and cut it in half, putting up the wood and dropping everything down to make it a mini-locker. Then I got some doweling and sawed it so it fit into the little locker, giving him a place to hang clothes. I also got some nails and put up a board so he would have a place to put his shoes.

The whole thing, when finished, couldn't have been more than three feet high. Then I pounded in some more nails so he would have a place to hang his socks, jock, and ball cap.

Now came the *coup de grace:* I put his name on a little piece of tape, just like over a real locker, and I got a little baby stool and set it inside the locker. Even the stool was cut down. It was beautiful—a baby locker, completely equipped. Just like it was for Billy Barty.

Now everybody was waiting for Penguin to arrive. He got there at about 9:00 A.M., walked up to his locker as usual, and just froze. He just stood there staring at it, his eyes going up and down. Then he stepped back, looked at it again, and started shaking his head. By now guys were rolling on the floor, almost crying, and Jerry Reuss is chirping in a high voice, "Penguin . . . Penguin," It was a triumph.

I loved to aggravate Cey, too, about his overbite. Once I got a bale of hay and put it in his locker, along with a note that read: "Dear Ronnie: The producers of the 'Mr. Ed' television show would like to welcome you to the Chicago Cubs and present you with this gift."

One other time I got a giant toothbrush with four-inch bristles, the kind they use to clean horses' teeth, and hung it in the locker.

I was merciless—like the time in Pittsburgh, about a month and a half into the season. It was Ronnie's first year with the Cubs, and he was really feeling the pressure. He had been hitting the ball hard—I mean really smoking it— but nothing was falling. He couldn't buy a hit, and nothing frustrates a hitter more. He's ripping line drives, and his batting average is about .118. There had also been a lot of wind blowing in from the outfield that spring in Chicago, and Pengy must have hit a half dozen balls that would have been home runs if they hadn't blown back.

So now we're in Pittsburgh, and Mooch, the clubhouse man, found me a mannequin. It was just the head, shoulders, and body—no legs. So I sit it on a little stool in front of Penguin's locker and put Cey's jersey on it. Then I get his pants and tuck the legs into his shoes under the mannequin and place a ball cap on the head. Finally, I put a little scarf around the neck, and under the sleeve I put a baseball bat. It was a work of art.

You should understand, now, that we're in the middle of a long losing streak. Penguin wasn't the only guy strug- gling. Everybody needed to relax a little. So I go into my act. I start walking up and down in front of this mannequin in front of Cey's locker, and I'm giving him my Knute Rockne pep talk.

"You've got to hang in there, Ronnie," I'm saying. "Those line drives you been hittin' will start to fall in . . . and don't worry about that wind, Ronnie, because one of these days it'll start blowing the other way. Don't hang your head, Ronnie. Hang in there. Don't give up. We all know you're striking out a lot but don't worry. After a while the ball will at least hit your bat."

All this time, of course, I'm walking up and down and talking to the mannequin. The other players are falling down and giggling, but Cey doesn't hear me. He's in the training room whirlpool.

Now he comes out with that distinctive Penguin strut, and he sees me giving the speech. Meanwhile, Dallas Green, the general manager, is in manager Lee Elia's office, watching. He's laughing so hard that he has to kick the door closed because he doesn't want the other players to see him. The boss isn't supposed to be laughing when his team has lost eight or nine in a row.

Penguin, meanwhile, just stands there with a towel around him, looking down at the mannequin. Finally, he just starts shaking his head, mumbles a few words to me and himself, turns around, and walks right back into the training room.

It gave us all a good laugh when we needed it. And you know what? We lost that game, too, but finally those line drives did start to fall, and the wind did start blowing out at Wrigley Field, as it always does when the hot weather arrives.

This, too, about Ron Cey: Most ball players would have buckled under the pressure he was under when he first went from the Dodgers to the Cubs. He didn't. He took abuse, but he stood his ground. Then, in 1984, he played much of the season with two injured wrists and still drove in 97 runs.

Pengy will fool you. Ex-major-leaguer Bill (Spaceman) Lee wrote in his own book, *The Wrong Stuff*, about the first time he pitched against Cey:

"Early in the game this little, bowlegged, gimpy guy got up to the plate and I thought, Jesus, do they expect this guy to hit me? I threw him a slider inside. Boom! Double off the left field wall. It was Ron Cey. I watched him slide into second base and thought to myself, Holy shit, imagine if this guy had two legs. I'd really be in trouble."

A lot of pitchers have been in trouble against Penguin.

But he was always in trouble when I was around. Anyway, he understands me, and he knows that I'm just trying to get him to lighten up. One night in Atlanta, after a bad game, he asked me to go have a drink with him. I knew then that something must really be bothering him. He really needed someone to talk with. We all have bad days and disappointments, but you've got to deal with them.

Talk about disappointments. One of the biggest disappointments of my 22-year pro baseball career is that somebody stole my Star Patrol helmet.

I could live with being traded and released. I could handle wearing eight major league uniforms—Angels, White Sox, A's, Phillies, Yankees, Cubs, Padres, Dodgers—in two different leagues. I could even handle the pressures of rooming with Jim Piersall; playing under Danny Ozark, Tom Lasorda, and Billy Martin; and trying to find new ways to terrorize Ron Cey.

But I really liked that Star Patrol helmet. Somebody had sent it to me. It had one antenna missing, and when it was on my head, I felt . . . sort of natural, you know? Then somebody ripped it off. Sometimes I think nothing is sacred and that the game of baseball has gone to hell.

You really do have to be a little crazy to play this game. I've been called everything from "Moon Man" and "Crazy Jay" to "My Favorite Martian" and "The Disappearing Man." I've been described as flaky, spacey, and a clown.

But I prefer to think of myself as a throwback to another era—one of a vanishing breed of ball players who find health, happiness, and a certain degree of satisfaction in throwing creamed pies and putting hot stuff in somebody's undershorts.

Laughter is conducive to winning. I believe it, and any good manager believes it. Without it, playing this little boys' game can get downright boring.

There is also the pressure. Don't let anyone ever tell you

it doesn't exist. We're human. We have our problems, too. Maybe the dishwasher doesn't work some days. Maybe the battery is dead on the car. Maybe your kids are sick or your wife is mad or the idiot neighbor keeps running the power mower at 8:00 A.M.

Yet ball players are expected to be above all that when they get to the park. They're supposed to put everything aside, including their own injuries, and give 100 percent at all times. Some can, but many cannot. Some guys take their personal problems with them to the ballpark. Others somehow shelve them and play the game, and those are the ones you have to admire.

I also admired guys like Mark Fidrych. Not only did he talk to baseballs; he talked to soap. He even got down on his hands and knees and wiped off the pitching rubber. I admired Moe Drabowsky, who made overseas phone calls from the bullpen telephone, and Doug Rader, who planted a cherry bomb in Jimmy Wynn's locker, lit a fire in a rowboat, and answered his front door in the nude. Those are my heroes. They, and a decreasing number of others like them, have also been holdouts against today's breed of million-dollar-contract-don't-take-any-chances-or-crack-a-smile ball players.

I don't think I act crazy at all. A little different? That's fair.

Basically, my behavior comes from a fear of failure—the fear of making a fool of myself in front of 50,000 people who expect excellence at all times. Everything we do as ball players is magnified and projected. Strike out in a World Series game and 50 million people are watching. You have pressure from team management, the media, your peers, the fans, and, most of all, the pressure put on by yourself.

Self-imposed pressure is the most difficult to deal with. No matter how well you can hit a baseball, for example, you're going to fail about 70 percent of the time even if you're great. I've always agreed with Ted Williams that it's the toughest thing to do in sports—hit a baseball thrown at 90 miles per hour—and when you fail, you have to know how to live with it.

Where else can one succeed only 30 percent of the time and be considered outstanding? Thirty percent in business, school, society, or almost anywhere else is considered failure.

Isn't there a country song about acting crazy to keep from going insane? Or maybe I'm thinking of Mel McDaniel's classic, "If You Keep On Goin' Crazy, You'll Get There, Bye and Bye." I suppose either song says a lot about why I act the way I do. But there really is a method to this madness.

Most managers want humor in the clubhouse. Tom Lasorda of the Dodgers, for example, said, "Jay, I want you to make my clubhouse funny. I want you to do whatever it takes to make the guys laugh."

"You mean anything?" I asked.

"Well, within reason," he said, and I could see he was already starting to worry.

I'm not sure that tying his squatty body in a room (more on this later) was within reason, but who's perfect? Basically, he gave me free rein to do whatever I wanted to do within the Dodger clubhouse. Perhaps I overstepped my bounds a few times (I don't think he liked it when we removed the desk from his office and installed a Hollywood makeup mirror), but everything was done in the best interest of the team—to make people laugh.

When I first came to the Dodgers in 1980 I heard about a severe morale problem from the year before, when they won only 79 games and lost 83, finishing third in the National League West. So I tried to do things where we would get maybe 12 to 15 guys involved. The more people involved, the more chance of unity and camaraderie. You literally get things going. You also look for the loners—

guys like pitcher Dave Goltz—who aren't accustomed to participating, and get them involved.

When I was with the Philadelphia Phillies (1974–78), we would hold cold duck parties. Tony Taylor and I would get a hotel suite and buy a supply of cold duck—not any hard liquor, just something with a little bite—and we'd invite only the players to come to the room for a general bullshit session. You know, bitches and gripes. Air it out. Once a month on the road we'd do it. Nobody *had* to show up, of course, but we strongly suggested that they make it—sort of a command performance to clear the air—and it really worked.

Even when things were going well, we'd do it. It was for the players. Somebody would pop a cork, stand in front of the room, and say, "OK, any bitches? Any gripes?" And if some outfielder was getting a little tired of the same infielder blowing the cutoff throw, he'd let him have it, right there. You play six to eight months a year with the same people and personality conflicts can really develop. You would be amazed at how little petty things can grow into major issues. So we would let it rip and throw it all out for discussion. Play a little music, tell a few jokes, maybe even hire a dancer or two, and, above all, have some laughs. I think the original idea with the Phillies came from Taylor and Richie Allen, and it worked. It helped us become a team.

We even got to the point where we had Paul Owens (Phillies' general manager) picking up the tab for $150 trays of hors d'oeuvres. He never once complained. He even encouraged it. It was cheap therapy.

So when I went to the Cubs (1982) and saw how serious those guys were (wouldn't you be serious if your franchise hadn't reached the World Series since World War II?), I talked with GM Dallas Green about doing the same thing. Fergy Jenkins and I tried it.

They weren't laughing a lot in those days at Wrigley

Field, though. Talk about a serious clubhouse—it was a morgue. When I first arrived, we were in the midst of a long losing streak, eight or nine games, I think. So I said to myself, "I gotta do something."

The first thing I noticed was that the coaches were really taking it hard. The manager, Lee Elia, was under a lot of pressure, and one of his coaches, John Vukovich—a man I really grew to like and admire—especially had a hard time accepting defeat. So after about the sixth straight loss I said to myself, "What is this? Everybody looks like their mother just died." So I went over to the jukebox and punched a button, and on comes Michael Jackson belting "Beat It" or something raucous, and heads started popping up all over the locker room. I know they thought I was nuts.

"What the hell!" I yelled. "So we lost. Does that mean the sun doesn't come up tomorrow? What's the matter with you guys?"

But about now, the coaches came running out of their own room. Vukovich slammed off the jukebox and yelled, "Who turned on that music? We don't like music when we lose!"

"Does that mean we're going to come back and lose again tomorrow?" I yelled back. "Are we gonna have to hang our heads forever?"

I really think I shook up a lot of people over there. Next thing I did was go out and buy 25 Superman T-shirts. Then I called a meeting—no coaches allowed—and handed out the shirts. They all had big red S's on them.

"If you wear these shirts," I said, "something is bound to happen."

Of the 25 guys, I think at least 20 wore their Superman T-shirts under their uniforms that night. We lost anyhow, but what the hell? We had some laughs. We also turned it around and had a big winning streak one week later. And some of the Cubbies still have those shirts. I saw a locker room picture of Ryne Sandberg wearing his during the 1984 playoffs.

When you've been on as many clubs as I have, you see all kinds of personalities. You also see what can happen—how a situation can snowball. There are simply times when somebody needs to do something weird, maybe even asinine, to break the tension. I'm your guy.

However, there are times when even I wonder why I do the things I do.

Like the night Dodger relief pitcher Steve Howe got shelled, then heard the inevitable verbal shot from across the locker room: "Hey, Howser, you're supposed to put water on that fire, not gasoline."

Now, I could have left it alone. Instead, I slipped down to the groundskeepers' room and appropriated this giant, red, five-gallon gasoline can, which I hung in Howe's locker, with his name written on the can.

Howe came out of the shower, saw the can, and immediately got pissed off and started blaming Jerry Reuss, who had been kidding him earlier. This was perfect, as far as I was concerned. It's always more satisfying when somebody else gets blamed for your stuff. Anyhow, Reuss and Howe got into it pretty good, and finally Jerry, with his distinguished voice, said: "I had nothing to do with it, Howser, but it was a great idea, and you probably deserved it."

Now Howe, who has a rather bizarre sense of humor, the next day took Reuss's shoes into the john and did something totally disgusting to them—I can't tell you what—and put them back into Reuss's locker. The funny part is that he committed the dastardly act in the john right next to where Reuss was sitting and Reuss didn't know it.

This was a team, understand, that also had Rick Sutcliffe, and Reuss wasn't exactly sure whether Howe was guilty or not. Jerry, though, is a patient man. He went into a Sherlock Holmes bit to start eliminating suspects and finally—at least a couple of days later—decided for sure that the guilty party was Howe. We were on a road trip in Montreal, and he got Howe's hotel room number. He called room service, told the chef he wanted a special order for his fiancée, gave Howe's name and number, and ordered breakfast to be delivered the following morning— $110 worth of breakfast, everything from champagne, bacon, eggs, and pancakes to strawberries and melon.

Howe was still asleep, of course, when the room service guy knocked on his door at 6:00 A.M. with $110 worth of breakfast.

But after considerable discussion, he decided to accept the order, even though he got them to take back the champagne and roses. He then called Dave Stewart, Bobby Castillo, and a couple of other guys to help him eat it.

It's funny how things steamroll. All I did was bring in one gas can.

Howe, of course, has always been an easy target. Even back in 1980, when he was National League Rookie of the Year with 17 saves and a 2.65 ERA, Howser was cocky. And you know what happens to cocky rookies.

Once during spring training we ran all of his street clothes up the flagpole at Holman Stadium in Vero Beach, where the Dodgers play their exhibition games. Howe was already in uniform, and when he got to the stadium for calisthenics, he looked up to see his own underwear, socks, pants, and shirt flapping atop the pole.

Keeping one's clothes intact around a ball club is never an easy task. One time I went into the clubhouse during a game and cut the middle out of Sutcliffe's underwear. Then I made sure I wasn't sitting nearby after the game, when he started to get dressed. I've always savored that flash on a guy's face when he realizes something is wrong but can't figure out what. I mean there was big Rick pulling his shorts up, and they just kept right on going, all the way to his chest.

And, as often happens, he blamed it on somebody else, Don Stanhouse. Why? Because he had been laughing the hardest. He went over to Don Stanhouse's locker and started pulling all of his clothes out and throwing them onto the floor. Then he poured rubbing alcohol on them and set a match to the pile of clothes, right there in the locker room.

"What the hell . . . what the hell," is all Stanhouse could say when he saw his clothes on fire.

It was another triumph. By that time I was at the far end of the clubhouse, busy doing something else. Most guys, you see, want to be right there to gloat when they pull something. Not me. I just need a quick glimpse to make sure it's working. Then I get scarce. Sometimes I won't even be in the neighborhood. It's always better when somebody else gets blamed.

There have been times, of course, when I got caught. Sutcliffe, for example, eventually came after me, too. He took my expensive three-piece Polo suit, sank it into the whirlpool for a while, then put it into the large clothes dryer. By the time I got it back it had shrunk to Ron Cey's size. I should have had it pressed and sold it to the Penguin. But Sutcliffe stands 6'7" and has weighed as much as 240, so I really wasn't going to argue, but I had him looking over his shoulder for a while.

There have also been times when I wanted to be present for a confirmed kill but couldn't possibly be there. Like the time I put Capsolin in Dave Goltz's shorts. It is the hottest stuff ever to come out of a tube. But it's red, so if you want to use it and hide it, you need to disguise it. That's what I did with Goltz. I put the goo on my fingertips and rubbed it real good into the crotch of his shorts. Then I powdered the area so he wouldn't see the red.

The thing about Capsolin, too, is that it gets even hotter

when you cover it. Goltzy had no chance. He put on his street clothes and headed home to Cerritos, which is about 35 miles from Dodger Stadium. It was the fastest ride of his life.

He had his wife and baby in the car with him, and his wife couldn't figure out why he was driving so fast on the freeway. And when they reached the driveway, he jumped out of the car, leaving the door open and his wife and baby behind. By the time they got into the house, wondering what was wrong, Goltzy was already undressed and in the shower, balls ablaze.

Another favorite of mine is lining up guys for fictitious television interviews. At Dodgertown, for example, Tom Lasorda almost always allows his players to sleep in on Sunday mornings during spring training. It's a perfect setup. On Saturday night, we got some of publicity man Steve Brener's stationery and wrote these official notes to some of the young guys new with the club. Then we put the notes in their lockers on Saturday evening.

"Mike [Marshall] and Steve [Sax]," the note would read, "David Hartman of 'Good Morning America' will be in camp Sunday. Could you please represent the Dodgers on his show Sunday morning? Please be in full uniform by 8:00 A.M. and meet his crew outside the clubhouse. Thanks. Steve."

I'm almost always sleeping when the kids show up for their national TV debuts. So how could I be guilty?

But there are times when you can't hide. You've got to be there to make things happen.

Certainly I had to be present one spring with the Cubs in Mesa, Arizona, for the annual lecture on drug abuse. Cocaine was the subject this particular morning. We had George Kling, an FBI agent and friend of mine, and a guy from the Drug Enforcement Agency. Serious stuff. So just as they're beginning to warn us about the evils of cocaine, I started shaking and sneezing into my hand and blowing white powder all over the place. It was all over my nose, and these guys looked like they wanted to kill me. But they were the only guys in the place not laughing. It was just baby powder, so what was the big deal?

Considering what a serious problem drug abuse has become in sports, I suppose I should treat the subject more tactfully, because I'm dead against it. For some reason, though, I've always felt the athletes were the victims. All of our careers we have been given pills, analgesics, anti-inflammatory drugs, painkillers, uppers, whatever—all to keep us on the field when perhaps we should have been on a training table or in a hospital bed. Frankly, I'm amazed that more professional athletes haven't had serious drug problems. Maybe it's *because* they're pros that they're able to deal with it.

We are humans. Many people understand that; more don't. We make human mistakes—sometimes because we can't handle the pressure, whether it comes from within or outside. Consider the case of pitcher Dave Stewart of the Texas Rangers. Helluva guy. I don't know anybody in baseball who doesn't like Stew and that high-pitched squeaky voice of his. But Dave went into the 1985 season under a lot of self-imposed pressure. He was arrested during the off-season in downtown Los Angeles and charged with lewd conduct. It seems he was caught in a parked automobile in a compromising position with a girl who wasn't a girl. It was a transvestite named Lucille. Stew, of course, didn't know until the cops told him. He hadn't gotten that far.

So when he showed up at spring training with the Rangers, how did his teammates handle this sensitive subject?

The first thing they did on the first day was sing, in unison: "You picked a fine time to leave me, Lucille."

Stew made a human mistake. But Stew is also a ball player, and that means he lives in a pressurized fishbowl.

And as my pal Jerry Reuss says: "He's got the best move in baseball with a man on."

"

My first major league roommate was Jimmy Piersall. That explains everything, right?

"

CHAPTER

2

HEY, SOME OF MY BEST FRIENDS ARE CRAZY

"He roomed with Piersall, hid from Danny Ozark, locked up Tom Lasorda, and dragged the infield with me. If there's anyone who is a product of his environment, it's Jay Johnstone."

Jerry Reuss

Jerry Reuss is a very serious person. He is serious about the business of pitching (60 victories for the Dodgers over a four-year period, 1980–84) and has been both a representative and a consultant for the Major League Baseball Players Association. He is a tall (6'5"), imposing, sometimes grim-faced man with an albino mustache and piercing eyes.

He is also wacko. I suppose that's why we get along. There are times when we don't have to say a word to communicate. We just look at each other and know. We are on a bus trip during spring training one year, for example, and as I come back to talk with him, he looks up from whatever he's reading and has sort of a demented grin on his face.

I just start laughing, and when I start laughing, he starts laughing. It becomes contagious. Now we've got guys

17

laughing all over the bus, and neither of us has said a word. I mean we're starting to cry we're laughing so hard, and you can hear other guys asking, "What did they say?" Then they start laughing, too, and they don't have any idea why. It was hilarious. Finally, I went back to my seat, and there must have been a dozen guys back there laughing. Jerry and I still hadn't even spoken.

Now it's about a month later, during the season, and I come into the clubhouse, and Reuss is leaning over the pass list. I walk up to put my name on the list, and as he looks up he's got that same demented grin. Once again, I start laughing. And this time he says, "This could be the day, huh? Something has got to happen today."

So I go into the outfield to shag fly balls, and he comes up and says, "Well, whattaya want to do? This has got to be the day." I think the moon might have been full. Why else would we decide to drag the infield?

Just before the fourth inning we slipped down to the groundskeepers and said, "We're gonna drag the infield. Two guys want to go along?"

They thought it was a great idea. Two got the night off, and the other two could go home and tell their wives how loony ball players are.

First we have to change into their clothes. Now we're waiting down in that little room off the dugout tunnel, and nobody is missing us. Then, when the fifth inning is finished, we run real quickly into the dugout, grab the stuff, and head toward third base with the other two guys.

But we don't quite go undetected. Rick Monday is standing at the end of the dugout and spots us just as we reach the third base line. So he walks to the dugout phone and calls the guy upstairs who runs Diamond Vision, that huge television screen above the left field pavilion. Maybe by now some other people know something is different, too. Normally there are four black guys out there working; now we look like an Oreo cookie. And it wasn't really that easy either. The hardest part was trying to walk like one of those guys—you know, swagger—and still drag the infield. We kept jerking the thing, that long, metal trellis they use to take the cleat marks out of the dirt.

By the time we reach the shortstop portion of the infield, Diamond Vision's camera has picked us up. It zooms in on the grounds crew, and there is Reuss's blond hair sticking out from his cap. And by the time we reach second, we've got 47,000 people watching. Some are starting to applaud, and the rest are wondering what in hell is going on.

When we finish (we did nice work, actually), we put down that big lattice and other tools along the first base side and follow the regular groundskeepers up the aisle behind home plate and through the crowd. Reuss is now tipping his cap, and we're getting an ovation.

But when we get back to the dugout, Lasorda says, "It'll cost you both $200 for being out of uniform."

Now, too, we have to walk all the way down to the batting cage behind the dugout tunnel to change back into our uniforms. And I start to worry. I know Lasorda.

"I've got to hurry," I tell Jerry. "That SOB will probably want me to pinch-hit or something."

"Nah," says Jerry. "Don't be silly."

But I'm changing fast. I'm trying to get my pants on and my shoes on at the same time and getting all tangled up. I just have a feeling.

And sure enough, I hear him yelling, "Where the fuck is Johnstone?"

Now I'm yelling, "I'm here, I'm here," as I run through the tunnel with my belt flapping, and when I turn the corner there's Lasorda, yelling, "Get up there and hit for the pitcher."

I'm out of breath, but I know he's not kidding. Our starting pitcher, Burt Hooton, has been having arm problems, and this was a perfect way for Tommy to burn me.

But this was my night. I hit a 2-1 pitch over the right field fence for a home run. And as I come back into the dugout, it's bedlam. Guys are rolling around hysterical on the floor, and Lasorda is in shock. The other coaches, particularly Monty Basgall, are turning away to keep Tommy from seeing they are laughing.

Now I'm shaking everybody's hand, and when I get to Lasorda, I nudge him and say, "Hey, Tommy, next time you need me, I'll be down in the groundskeepers' room."

And we never did pay those $200 fines. In fact, people got such a kick out of the whole thing that they were sending in donations to help pay the fines. We donated them to a hospital in Orange County.

That was appropriate, inasmuch as Reuss and I occasionally liked to play doctor. We'd get the Dodger doctor's note pad and send a note to a player, something like "Due to the fact that there was an abnormality in your urine sample, please bring us another."

Steve Sax and Davey Lopes both fell for it. Lopes goes into the doctor and says, "OK, what have I got, Doc? Tell me. Is it a disease or what?"

Mad Doctor Reuss also conned several guys into bringing in sperm samples. Can you imagine walking into a clubhouse with a sperm sample and all your teammates sitting there laughing and asking how you got it? I told you nothing was sacred.

My favorite medical gag, though, came one day at the Dodgertown dispensary during spring training.

Instead of a urine sample, I had filled my vial with apple juice from the Dodgertown cafeteria. Then I walked into the dispensary and placed it in front of the nurse.

"Gee, that's awfully cloudy," she said.

"Yeah, it sure is," I answered. "Here, let me run it through again."

With that, I chugalugged the apple juice, and the nurse started screaming.

"Wait right here," I said. "I'll run out and bring another sample back. Should just take a second."

By now, she had lost her glasses. I was afraid she might have a heart attack. The doctor really got mad at me because she was elderly. In fact, she retired soon after that. Maybe she figured she'd seen it all.

Reuss, of course, was a co-conspirator in our various Green Hornet escapades. We can't claim originality. Jimmy Lefebvre had apparently used the anonymity of the Hornet for pranks of his own over the years at Dodgertown. But in training camp of 1981—the year of the strike and year of the last Dodgers' world championship—I decided it was time for a Hornet revival.

I enlisted Reuss, Stanhouse, and—believe it or not—Mr. Clean himself, Steve Garvey. We got green cans of paint, and I hung a big sheet on the backstop of practice field number two, located just behind the clubhouse. On it was sprayed in green, "The Green Hornet Is Back."

From then on, whenever somebody wanted to harass somebody else—usually Lasorda—we would leave a green calling card. Stanhouse once slipped into Lasorda's room and sprayed a big green *G* on his bed sheet. We were spraying shoes green, anything we could get our hands on. And nobody really knew who was doing it because once in a while we'd spray something of our own, just to keep the Hornet's identity secret. Somehow, though, I have a feeling that Lasorda suspected Reuss, Stanhouse, and me. But Garvey? How could you suspect somebody with hair that never got mussed?

Reuss, incidentally, is a great actor. As long as he can keep from laughing, he can pull off almost anything. But once he starts giggling, forget it.

Stanhouse and I got him giggly once in Montreal. We were having a rain delay, and the grounds crew had the tarp out—not on the field yet, but out there ready to go, with the rope nearby. That's what caught our eyes—the rope. So Reuss was in the outfield doing his stretching exercises, and I walk up and say, "Whatcha doing?"

"Nothing," he says, but even as he spoke, he knew he was in trouble.

We get the tarp rope and start tying him up, and he starts

laughing. He's like Jello. Now we've got the rope, and he's helpless. We just keep wrapping and wrapping, and he's starting to look like a mummy. And it's five minutes before the game is going to start. Players are running past, getting loose, and there's Reuss on the ground, where we leave him, wrapped up like Houdini before an escape trick. But there is no way he can escape.

Finally a grounds crew guy goes out and says, "Can we have our rope back?"

Reuss answers, "Gee, I'm sorry, but I'm all tied up right now."

Next thing I know the umpires are out and it's time for the national anthem, and Reuss is still wrapped like a mummy in the outfield. Now they've got him on television and nobody can start anything until somebody goes out to untie him. It was wonderful. When you get the big albino laughing, you can do anything to him.

Yet, as I mentioned, Jerry is also one of baseball's better actors. Perhaps it's because of his "game face"—the term athletes use to describe their level of concentration before competition. Reuss has a fantastic game face. When he sits in front of that locker before pitching, it is no time for any visitor, or even a teammate, to wander up and ask how he feels about the designated hitter rule. Reuss has a laser glare.

That's why he's always so effective as a principal player in one of baseball's better one-act clubhouse routines, the Strongman Stunt.

I don't know where it started or when, but more than one innocent victim in more than one major league clubhouse has fallen prey to the Strongman. With the Dodgers, I suspect the routine was a little more elaborate. You tend to be that way with Lasorda around. Example: the way we indoctrinated Jim Bush, former UCLA track coach, during spring training, 1985, at Dodgertown, Vero Beach, Florida.

Lasorda began the ruse by calling for a closed-door

clubhouse meeting, but informing players that a TV camera crew would be allowed to tape his remarks. Nobody thought much about it. Lasorda is always talking into some kind of camera.

So he began by asking if anybody had any bitches or complaints. Reuss immediately stood and complained that he had lost $2,000 the year before in spring training wagering that he could lift three men at one time. He now pleaded for a chance to win back his money, obviously feeling strong enough to try again. Lasorda immediately ruled that he could have the opportunity. And immediately players began whipping out hundred-dollar bills and placing bets. Terry Whitfield jumped on top of the clubhouse table and started covering all bets. No way, said Whitfield, could Reuss possibly lift three men at one time. Before you knew it, money was everywhere and Bush, who had just joined the club as a special running instructor for spring training, was aghast.

"Are you sure you want to do this?" said Bush, an expert on physical conditioning. "You could really strain yourself."

Reuss assured Jim that he had devised a new and improved technique. He would have all three men lie flat on the floor, faces up, with their arms and legs interlocked. Then Reuss was to bend down and do his lifting.

Everybody in the clubhouse, of course, knew about the Strongman routine but Bush. He was the designated victim. Newcomer Al Oliver had been suggested, but somebody realized that Al had probably taught Reuss the trick in the first place when they both played in Pittsburgh with the Pirates. So Bush was the target.

"We need three volunteers," said Reuss, and immediately instructor Joe Ferguson and coach Mark Cresse volunteered. Inasmuch as each weighs more than 200 pounds, it was quickly decided that the third volunteer should weigh less to make Reuss's herculean task easier.

Would Bush please help? How could the new fellow refuse?

So Bush went flat on his back, wedged and interlocked between Ferguson and Cresse. Lasorda, meanwhile, had decreed that Reuss would win the wager if a baseball could be rolled on towels under the soon-to-be-raised backs of the three men. Tommy had been on his hands and knees, practice-rolling the ball over the towels, while others continued to argue and wager. Pedro Guerrero, who had signed a five-year contract worth $7 million just the year before, was now operating a loan shark office, offering short-term money at 10-percent interest.

Finally, the three volunteers were in place. And as Bush lay there, unable to move because he was held firmly on both sides, he still wasn't suspicious. He said one more time: "Jerry, please don't get hurt." It wasn't until he looked up and saw Reuss standing over him, with hands clasped and eyes closed in meditation, that he finally realized he had been had.

It began with the unbuttoning of Bush's pants. Then the shirt was opened, and the deluge began—shaving cream, crushed bananas, juice, everything smeared all over his face and body. People were howling, the TV camera was rolling, and there wasn't a thing he could do.

Then came the smasher. Lasorda poured a warm, liquid substance over Bush's body.

"Have some warm tea," said Lasorda.

"Oh, no, not that," shouted pitcher Carlos Diaz. "You just poured my urine sample on him."

"I was sure it was his sample," said Bush afterward. "I had never felt more helpless in my life."

It wasn't urine, of course. What do you take us for, crass individuals? When Bush was finally released, in fact, Lasorda asked the players if they now felt he truly deserved to be called a Dodger. He got a rousing ovation.

The Strongman routine is a great one, but there's only one problem: You can only set up a person once.

Well, that's not exactly true either. Ex-Dodger Mickey Hatcher, now with the Minnesota Twins, was so naive that he fell for it twice.

The best thing about a good con, of course, is picking the right person to con. Lasorda is a constant target.

Consider the Pizza Caper. It came at the conclusion of a chartered Dodger flight from Los Angeles to Chicago. It is not a short flight. People get hungry. And during this flight, Reuss got hungry.

"Hey, Tommy," he said to Lasorda, "isn't Chicago a great pizza town?"

"The best," said Lasorda.

"It's too bad we don't know anybody with clout in Chicago," said Reuss. "Wouldn't it be great to have some pizzas waiting for us when we land?"

"Whattaya mean, no clout? You want pizza, I can get you pizza."

"No way," said Reuss. "In fact, I'll bet you $20 you can't have 20 pizzas waiting for us when we land."

"You'll pay me $20? You're easy, Reuss. Watch how a man with influence operates."

With that, Lasorda went into the front cabin, persuaded the pilot to radio ahead, and made arrangements with one of his Italian friends in Chicago.

And sure enough, when we taxied to a stop at O'Hare Field, a guy came on board with 20 hot pizzas. Lasorda was proud as a peacock.

"OK, Reuss, where's my $20?" he said.

"Right here," said Reuss, handing over the money. "Where else can a person buy 20 pizzas for $20 and get free delivery?"

He then proceeded to feed the entire plane.

One more story about my wacko friend. We were in the dugout one day, and Reuss was sitting next to Reggie Smith, chewing tobacco. Reggie did not like people to chew tobacco around him. He especially didn't like to have it spewed on him.

Reuss knew this, of course, and each time he spit on the ground he made sure a little got on Reggie. Then he'd quickly say, "Oh, Reg, look, I'm sorry. I really am sorry. I didn't mean to do it."

"Why don't you just get rid of that stuff?" said Reggie, and about that time Joe Ferguson hit a home run.

"OK, Reggie, just for you I will," said Reuss, and he rushed off to join others in congratulating Ferguson. Lasorda was there, too, and as Jerry walked past to shake Ferguson's hand, he dropped the chew of tobacco into Lasorda's coffee cup. Then he went back to his seat next to Reggie.

"What did you do with the chew?" said Reggie.

"I got rid of it," said Reuss.

"Where did you put it?"

"What difference does it make? I got rid of it."

Reggie, somewhat distrustful, kept looking around, afraid he might be sitting on it or something. And about that time, Lasorda took a drink of coffee and started gagging.

"Oh, no," said Reggie. "You didn't."

And Jerry says, "Yeah, I did."

Reuss may be wacko, but no more so than my first major league roommate.

My first major league roommate was Jimmy Piersall.

That explains everything, right?

I'll never forget that first day of Angels' spring training camp, 1967. I showed up in early afternoon, two suitcases in hand, and the door to the room was open.

"Hi, I'm Jay Johnstone," I said, standing at the door.

"Yeah, I know," said Piersall. "Let's get one thing straight."

"OK," I said, barely five feet inside the door.

"I'm the captain of the room," he said.

"Fine."

"What I watch on TV you watch on TV. When I go to bed, you go to bed. When I get up, you get up. Any questions so far?"

Now understand, I'm 20 years old and green as grass. I'm still standing there holding the suitcases. Am I going to argue?

"I don't smoke," said Piersall, "so you don't smoke. If you do smoke, you smoke outside. Smoke bothers me. And by the way, I like chocolate ice cream. If you can have a little pint of chocolate ice cream in the refrigerator after each game, I'd appreciate it."

"Hey," I finally said. "No problem. Rules are rules. I'm just glad to be here."

Jimmy ran at a pretty fast pace in those days. He'd get picked up by limos and members of the opposite sex at night and come home in the morning. I was in awe, but I was a good roomie. Chocolate ice cream was always in the refrigerator.

Jim gave me one piece of advice I have never forgotten.

"It's OK to get your name in the newspapers," he said, "so long as you don't disgace yourself or hurt anybody else. Keep your name out there. Let people know who you are. Let them read about you."

Certainly they were reading about Jimmy. But he'd just laugh and say, "I've got them all on the run. They think I'm crazy because I act crazy. But I'm not crazy. I've got papers to prove it."

My favorite Piersall story with the Angels came from Yankee Stadium, late in the 1962 season. Jimmy was with his third team that season, having started the year with the Washington Senators, then going to the New York Mets before coming to the Angels. He was playing center field for the Angels this day, and Ted Bowsfield, who told me the story, was pitching against the Yankees. But it was disaster.

Everything that Bowsfield threw to the plate came back about 100 miles per hour. It was one of those days. If our manager, Bill Rigney, had gone to the catcher to ask about

Bowsfield's stuff, the catcher would have probably answered "I don't know yet, I haven't caught one." I mean everything he threw turned into a rocket. We were losing 9–2 by the fifth inning, and our outfielders were getting worn out, running from gap to gap, chasing those line drives between the monuments. Those were the days when there was no fence around the monuments the Yankees had in the outfield to honor their all-time greats— Babe Ruth, Miller Huggins, and Lou Gehrig. The monuments were part of the playing field—deep in the outfield, to be sure, but nevertheless part of the field.

Well, by the fifth inning Piersall felt he had run down enough line drives. He disappeared. The umpires couldn't start the inning because the Angels didn't have a centerfielder. Finally, Rigney came running out of the dugout. He had spotted Jimmy in the outfield, hunched down behind one of those monuments, hiding. So Rigney had to walk into the outfield to see what was the matter.

"Look," said Jimmy. "I've got nine kids. There ain't no way you're gonna get me to play anymore with that guy pitching. He's gonna get somebody killed, and I got too many kids to support. Either take him out of the game or I ain't comin' out from behind this rock."

Rigney took Bowsfield out of the game.

I appeared on Piersall's TV show in Chicago a couple of years ago. We had some fun.

But he was very upset with me back when I hit my 100th home run two years ago with the Cubs. He felt I should have run around the bases backward. Actually, the only reason I didn't was that it had been a tight game and my homer made it 1–0. Ed Lynch was pitching for the Mets and throwing a helluva game, a one-hitter. I just didn't want to show him up. If it had been a lopsided score, I would have done a handstand at second base, then gone into cartwheels. But I didn't want to blow it for the kid, my home run being the only run.

I was fined $100, incidentally, for hitting that 100th home run because I swung on a 3-0 pitch. I was 5 for 5 when I swung at 3-0 pitches that season with the Cubs. That wasn't the dumbest fine I ever got, though. Jim Bunning, my manager for a few months in Toledo (1974), once fined me $50 for a base hit because the bat broke in half and I carried my half to first base with me. Bunning would fine guys $10 for missing signs, too. In those days, he was warped. He tried to be a perfectionist, but everybody can't be like me.

Maybe if Piersall had known I was fined $100 for that 100th home run, he would have been more understanding. Or, perhaps he should have remembered that advice he gave me 18 years before: Don't disgrace yourself or hurt anybody else.

Did knowing Jim Piersall when I was a rookie breaking into the game influence my behavior? Certainly I didn't consciously emulate him. Who would? But don't we get a little rub-off from many of the people we meet? Don't forget that I also played during those early years with people like Bo Belinsky, Jim Fregosi, Dean Chance, and George Brunet, the Angel who once missed the team plane, stole a taxi, and intercepted the plane on the runway before it could take off. The plane stopped, Brunet got on, and he left the taxi abandoned on the runway.

Would a ball player do that today? Nah. He'd go buy his own plane.

In those days, of course, there were more restrictions. Curfew meant something. Traveling secretaries and coaches spent most of their late hours worrying about who was in a ball player's hotel room and whether he was alone. Nowadays, for the most part, they don't care. Tommy Ferguson, traveling secretary for years with the Angels and Milwaukee Brewers (before becoming vice president), likes to tell about two major changes in his duties over the years.

"I always had to worry about curfew and salary advance

slips when we were on the road," said Fergy. "Players were always running out of cash, and I'd give them an advance on their salary. But what modern player needs a salary advance? The only guys who borrow money anymore are the sportswriters."

Ferguson, incidentally, now scouts for the Philadelphia Phillies.

"When Cleveland became New York and New York became Cleveland," said Ferguson, "I decided it was time to get off the road."

Curfew, money, and Bo Belinsky gave me the biggest scare of my rookie year. And if you're guessing that women were involved, you're right.

It was about 11:55 P.M., five minutes before midnight curfew, on the second floor of the Hilton Riviera in Palm Springs, where the Angels stayed. I was walking back to my room—minding my own business, believe it or not—when I saw Belinsky coming down the hall with these two gorgeous girls on his arms. I was stunned. There was an automatic $500 fine for any player who got caught with a girl in his room, and here was Bo with two, heading for his room, which was just three doors down from me. I was rooming at the time with Joey Amalfitano. (All the veterans, you see, wanted to room with me because I had a car. A blue and white Thunderbird. That's why I always got invited to go along at night. I got to drive. I didn't even realize that's why they wanted me. I thought they were just being nice, inviting me out. Hell, I wasn't even old enough to drink, but they would always say, "Don't worry, kid. We'll get you inside. Just sit there and have a good time." And all the time I was the transportation.)

Well, anyhow, here came Bo, and as soon as he saw me he said, "Hey, kid, take these girls down to the bar and buy them a drink for me. I've got to pick up something at the front desk."

"Oh, I can't."

"Whattaya mean, you can't?"

"Well, I just can't . . . uhhh, I'm not old enough to drink."

"Oh, yeah. Well, then take them into my room for a minute. I've got a bottle in there. Buy them a drink in my room. I'll be right back."

With that, he turned and left. And there I was—a rookie earning exactly $7,000 a year—facing a $500 fine. It was now two minutes to curfew. But like any red-blooded baseball rookie, I took them into the room. I was trying to make conversation and pour them a drink, but I was sweating bullets. I started wondering if getting caught with two girls would mean two $500 fines. Was I sitting there looking at $1,000 of my $7,000 salary about to fly out the window? I didn't care how beautiful they were because I just knew one of the coaches was gonna be knocking on that door. They had coaches staying at the ends of each floor, with the traveling secretary at the other end and the manager on the bottom floor. Come in late and you had people watching at the only two places you could get upstairs.

But just as I was about to faint, Bo returned. It was now about 12:15 A.M., and he said, "Thanks, kid. I appreciate this a lot. Anything I can do for you? Want to go out with us?"

"You're going where?" I asked.

"Out," said Bo. "The night is still young."

I couldn't get back to my room fast enough. I just sat on my bed, shaking my head. But then I went to the window and looked out into the parking lot and, sure enough, there was Bo, getting into this red Cadillac convertible. He was in the middle, with an arm around each girl (I later found out that one was Mamie Van Doren), and zzzzooom!, in a cloud of dust, they took off into the night.

Wow, I thought. This is really the big leagues.

Rookies have been fair game since the beginning of baseball. That's one part of the game that will never change. I've always wondered who A. G. Spalding picked on, or if he was as imaginative as some of my Angel teammates in the early '60s.

Consider the time Dean Chance introduced one of our young outfielders, Jack Warner, to both of his wives. Actually, neither was, but poor Jack had no idea.

The joke began when Dean asked Jack if he would like to bring his own young wife and join the Chances for dinner. Jack was honored. The two couples had a lovely dinner. The women got along famously, and Warner was thrilled that this veteran player would show him so much attention.

And when Jack told Dean the next day how much he and his wife had enjoyed the evening, Chance said, "We enjoyed it, too. In fact, how about dinner again tonight? I know another great place."

Warner accepted and showed up that evening at the restaurant with his wife. Chance was there, too, with a different woman than he had dined with the evening before. And he introduced her, too, as "Mrs. Chance."

They didn't go out a third time.

" Enter Benny Lefebvre. I would have been out of baseball 13 years ago if not for him. . . . And can you imagine how peaceful the last decade would have been for the Penguin and Lasorda? **"**

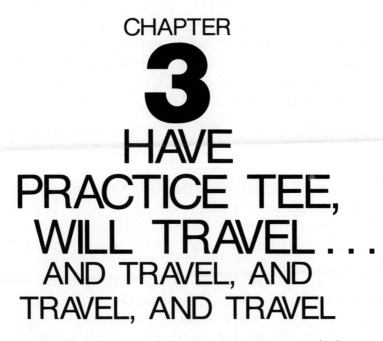

CHAPTER

3

HAVE PRACTICE TEE, WILL TRAVEL . . .
AND TRAVEL, AND TRAVEL, AND TRAVEL

"Don't blame me for Johnstone. He was crazy before I met him."

Jimmy Piersall

If you've read this far, you may be thinking that the way to succeed in major league baseball is to report to spring training every year with a load of lemon pies and smash one in somebody's face every day.

It's not quite that easy. You also have to play the game. You have to love to play the game, too—which I do. And while I don't think they'll ever have a plaque with my name on it in Cooperstown (not even a bronzed groundskeepers cap, in honor of hitting a home run one inning after dragging the infield), I certainly owe no apologies.

I can play. I can hit. And when you look at the numbers, which all self-respecting baseball fans do, you'll quickly notice that my batting average is considerably higher in the National League than in the American. There's a good reason for that. First, though, the numbers prior to the 1985 season:

- Major league lifetime batting average: .267
- American League lifetime batting average: .248
- National League lifetime batting average: .289, including those back-to-back seasons, 1975 and 1976, when I hit .329 and .318 with the Phillies

I was also fortunate enough to be able to contribute to pennant-winning and world championship teams—and winning is always the bottom line with any athlete, amateur or professional, no matter what the sport.

We won divisional titles with the Phillies in 1976 and 1977, and in that three-game playoff that we lost against the Cincinnati Reds in 1976 I set a league championship playoff series hitting record of .778.

It's easier to hit .778, of course, when you bat only 9 times. But I'll take 7 for 9 anytime, anywhere. It just made it sweeter that it came in the playoffs. Nice number, .778, isn't it? You can look it up. It would have been 8 for 9 if Dave Concepcion hadn't robbed me of a hit to center field.

My two World Series rings came from the New York Yankees (1978) and Los Angeles Dodgers (1981). Final postseason hitting statistics:

- League championship series: .500 (8 for 16)
- World Series: .667 (2 for 3)
- Total postseason: .526 (10 for 19)

Highlights? Anyone with major league service time of 16 years and 52 days (prior to the 1985 season) has to have had a few.

Dodger fans, I suppose, remember best my pinch home run off Ron Davis of the Yankees in the fourth game of the 1981 World Series. It wasn't as dramatic as that shot in the final playoff game in Montreal by Rick Monday—the swing of the bat that got us into the Series—but mine was a biggie nevertheless. It was a two-run blast (I love that word, *blast*) that helped the Dodgers win, 8–7, as we came back from a 2–0 game deficit to beat the Yankees in six.

Yankee owner George Steinbrenner was so mad after that game that he came into the locker room screaming at Davis. The Yankees, up 2–1 in games, had led us, 4–0 and 6–3, in game four, only to blow it. My homer brought us from 6–3 to 6–5. That's the game, too, when Reggie Jackson tried to catch a fly ball with his shoulder instead of his glove. It's no wonder George was mad.

But I had to laugh when I heard that he screamed at Davis, "Why did you throw Johnstone a fastball?"

Davis is a fastball pitcher. That's all he is. So what was he supposed to be throwing, a forkball?

That 1981 season, incidentally, was a good one for me as a pinch hitter with the Dodgers. I led the club with 11 pinch hits, just four short of the club record, for a .289 average (11 for 38), and had three pinch-hit home runs. At last look, I was 12th on the major league all-time list as a pinch hitter and 11th on the all-time list for pinch-hit home runs.

So baseball's been good to me. I'm telling you this because I don't want to sound sacrilegious—critic of the Great National Pastime, biter of the hand that feeds me, etc.—but I have to say that this is a very superficial thing that we do for a living.

Consider the life-style of a professional baseball player: One day he's here and a hero; the next day he's there and forgotten.

Perhaps that is why I don't have many good friends that are ball players. Sure, there are guys I enjoy being with and with whom I've kept in contact. Some have remained good friends beyond baseball. But in a way, it's a little like the buddy system in combat (though less lethal). One day your pal is using the locker next to you. The next day he's traded or released and it's "Oh, aaah, hey, good luck . . . see you down the road."

It's almost always awkward, especially when a guy trying to make the team in spring training gets cut. You don't know what to say, so you look for places to go. I've even hidden in the training room, hoping the guy will be gone before I come out, because there was really nothing I could say to him.

It's almost as if there's an inner feeling that says, "I'm glad it's him and not me."

As many teams as I've been with—nine, if you count the spring Charlie Finley loaned me to the St. Louis Cardinals—I've seen a lot of guys come and go. I've been released four times and traded three times myself. Believe me, it's never easy.

So the friendships are often shallow ones. You spend a lot of time together—sometimes six, seven months of real close relationship. The guy can even be your roommate. But if you live on the West Coast and he lives on the East Coast, you split when winter comes and you don't see him until the following spring. Maybe a Christmas card, maybe not. Maybe neither of you will even pick up the phone. Then comes spring, and it's like you haven't been away. It's weird, actually. It's like "Hey, let's go to dinner" as if you just saw him yesterday. Or maybe you won't see him the following spring at all. Maybe one of you was traded. That's baseball. Gulliver, that great traveler, would have been a great ball player if he could have hit the curve.

There is only one way to look at being traded and preserve your sanity. If I'm traded, it means I'm going to a club that wants me. And my usefulness to the team that traded me has ended, so I don't want to hang around. It's really that simple.

The first time I was traded was the toughest. Other ball players have told me the same thing. It's that first real jolt: Somebody doesn't want me.

In my case, I didn't want to go. I had been with the California Angels' organization since turning pro in 1963, right out of Edgewood High School in West Covina, California. Now, seven years later—after those pit stops in San Jose ($3-a-day meal money), El Paso, and Seattle—I was

That's Mickey Mantle on the right. The way I remember it, he just wanted my autograph.

Just two little Angels, circa 1967: rookie Johnstone and his roomie Jimmy Piersall.

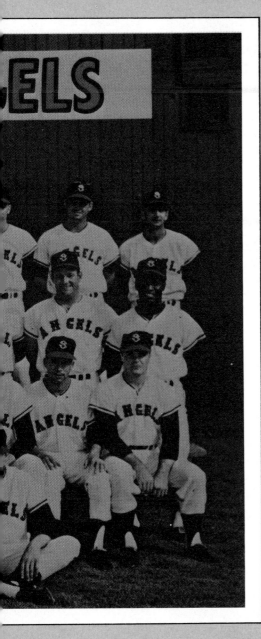

Jim Bouton and yours truly, 1967: minor leaguers and aspiring authors.

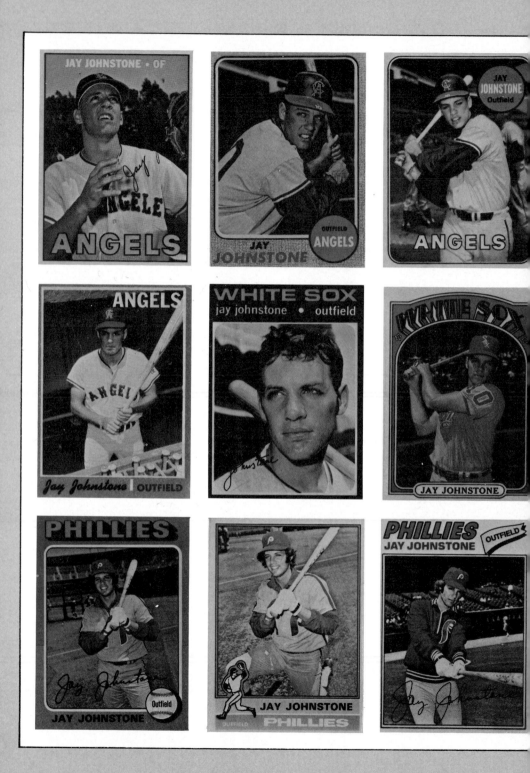

Mary Jayne Sarah
Johnstone leads.
I just follow.

This is Mary Jayne.
She spelled it
that way before
Jayne Mansfield.

How could they ask an innocent face like this to take a 20 percent pay cut?

Umpire Jerry Crawford kneels to beg forgiveness for calling me out.

How did I tag out base runner Frank Taveras from right field? It wasn't exactly poetry.

Whaddaya mean,
rain delay? Let's go!

Sometimes you have to deceive the pitcher
to get that crucial hit.

No matter how lousy the swing, I can always manage a smile for the camera.

I didn't mind the pinstripes. It was the zoo keeper who bothered me.

From left, Bucky Dent, Dick Tidrow, Graig Nettles, Paul Lindblad, and me in the Yankee clubhouse—before we all broke out of the Bronx Zoo.

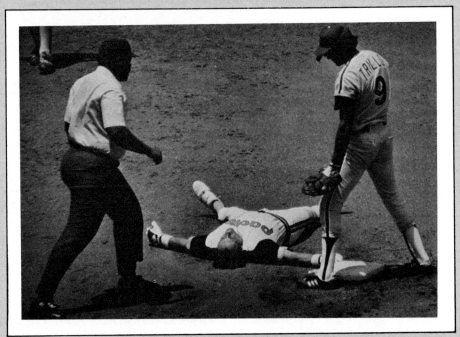

Umpire Charlie Williams and Manny Trillo insist that second base is no place for me to be working on my tan.

Hey, Tommy, I was just tryin' to help out.

Don Stanhouse, The Good Guy, and Jerry Reuss—would these sweet-lookin' guys try to cause trouble?

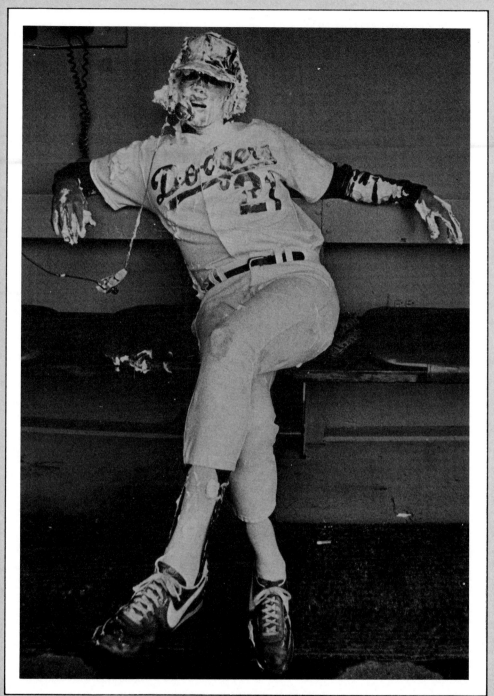

"Yeah, this is Johnstone. No, nothing much going on here. How 'bout you?"

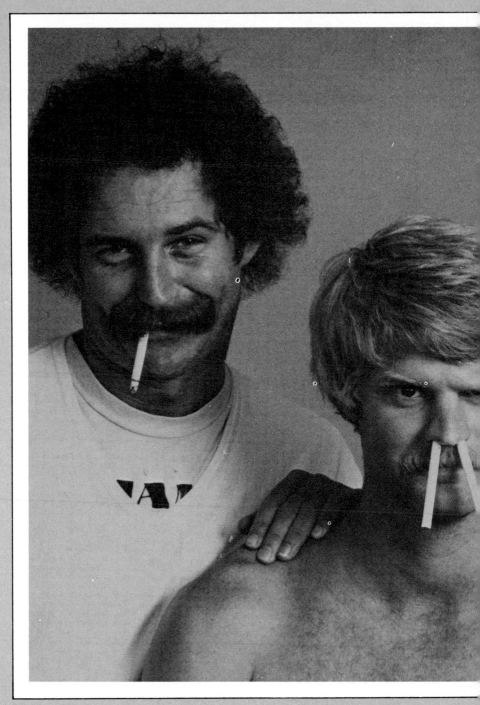

I'll never understand why Lasorda
was always nervous around us.

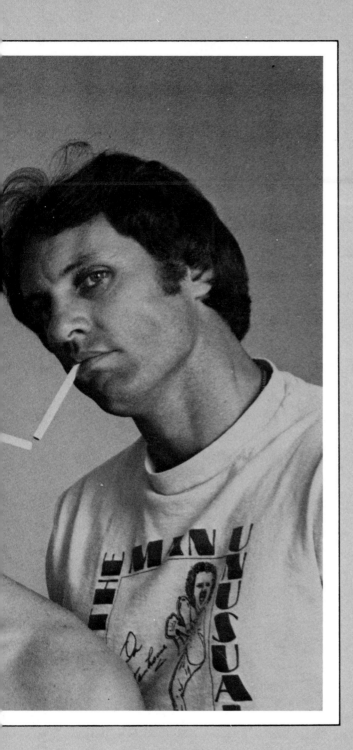

I don't know what was more exciting: winning this award
or getting to kiss sportswriter John Lowe.

being traded from the big club (Angels) to the Chicago White Sox.

Why me, Lord? Well, Roland Hemond and Chuck Tanner had both just gone from the Angels to Chicago—Hemond as personnel director, Tanner as field manager (the beginning of a managerial career that has yet to end for the "dean"). They wanted to rebuild with young players, and the first thing they did was swing a deal for some of the kids they'd known with the Angels. I was one of those kids.

I was also upset, even though Hemond, who now lives in the same town I live in (San Marino, California), had signed me on high school graduation night. Tanner, you see, had phoned me after he first got the job and said, "Jay, we're thinking about making a deal for you. We'd like you to play center field in Chicago. What do you think?"

"Gee, that's real flattering," I said, "but I'd rather stay in California, where my family and friends are."

Then, two weeks later, Hemond called and gave the same spiel. "Love to have you," he said.

"Sorry, Roland," I said. "I'd rather stay and play with the Angels. I told Chuck that two weeks ago."

"OK," said Hemond. "We understand."

About a week later they made the deal. Tom Bradley, Tom Egan, and I were to go to Chicago for three players—Sid O'Brien, Ken Berry, and Billy Wynne.

So much for asking me in the first place.

My Chicago White Sox experience was a roller coaster—.260 in 1971, with 16 home runs, then the uncomfortable role of player rep in 1972, a time when owners were trying to break the players' association. Hitting .188 in '72 didn't help either.

Enter Benny Lefebvre. I would have been out of baseball 13 years ago if not for him. Certainly I wouldn't be writing a book. And can you imagine how peaceful the last decade would have been for the Penguin and Lasorda?

My love affair with Lefebvre began in the winter of 1972.

And believe me, it didn't start any too soon. There is not a lot of demand for dazzling .188 hitters. Talk about careers on the rocks. You could have served mine with Stolichnaya and an orange slice and charged only 10 cents and still not have had any takers.

Understand, now, that I had been in the big leagues for seven seasons. I had 2,100 major league at-bats with the California Angels (1966–70) and White Sox (1971–72), and even though I did hit .270 with the Angels in 1969 (when I had 540 ABs), I was a career .245 hitter. The numbers don't lie. I've heard people describe baseball as an "island surrounded by a sea of statistics," but facts are facts. I was a career .245 hitter—a kid who could really go after the ball in the outfield—but I had just hit .188, and I knew how it felt to be booed on the south side of Chicago.

Welcome into my life, Benny Lefebvre. Not only did I not know how to spell his name, I had no idea who he was, until I met his son Jim at one of those off-season functions that ball players attend (ball players' translation of function: a free meal and a chance to get out of the house).

Jim had just finished the 1972 season with the Dodgers, and we started talking about hitting. More accurately, I started pouring my heart out about the problems I had in Chicago—249 at bats, 49 hits, 4 HRs, 17 RBIs, 42 strikeouts. Being a compassionate man, Jimmy listened and finally said, "We're working out every day. You're more than welcome to come work out with my dad and me."

"Gee," I said, "that's really nice."

But I'm thinking, "Why do I want to work out with this guy's dad? Who is his dad? Will his mother be coming along, too?" I knew little enough about Jim, inasmuch as he was in the National League and I was in the American.

On the other hand, what did I have to lose? Nobody has ever accused me of being afraid of work, and certainly this was a time of desperation. So on October 16, 1972, I showed up at 6:00 A.M. at this deserted high school gymnasium in Playa del Rey, California, to meet Benny Lefebvre and learn, all over again, how to hit a baseball.

It wasn't easy. In the first place, I had to leave my house in San Marino at 5:30 A.M. every day in order to reach the gym by 6:00 or 6:10. We had to work out so early because we had to be out of the gym before the first high school class started at 8:00 A.M. So we'd get there by 6:00, loosen up, do some exercises, and then start hitting tennis balls off the batting tee, just Jimmy and me, with his dad standing there.

So where was the miracle cure? No miracle. Just excruciating work . . . and the patience and mastery of a wonderful teacher, Benny Lefebvre.

He completely changed my swing. He altered my stance and got me to use my hips. I always thought I was a wrist hitter and should use my hands and arms. Well, you don't. You use your hips. Ted Williams teaches the same basic technique. Benny broke it down so simply that even a hard head like me could understand it. He even wrote a book about it.

Day after day, hour after hour, all winter long, we hit those tennis balls off batting tees. It's more or less a reflex drill—like hitting a whiffle ball. We'd set up the tee at midcourt of the gym, and the idea of a perfect swing was to hit a line drive and have it hit the center of the glass backboard. At first, we worked on only the basic fundamentals. Later, Benny would move the tee up and down.

Mostly, though, it was just repetition. Practice, practice, and practice. Talk about boring. A guy could go nuts spending an entire winter hitting tennis balls off a batting tee. He can also lose a lot of sleep getting up at 5:00 A.M. every day. But I had made up my mind. It was one of those soul-searching times when you look into the mirror and know that something will change in your life. Well, my baseball swing changed. It was as if I was no longer the same player who had been with the Angels and White Sox.

Finally, in February 1973, I started going down to St. Bernard Catholic High School where Benny was coaching. I worked with his kids. He had six batting tees set up and one guy hitting live pitching. The hitters would rotate—10 swings off the first tee, 10 off the second, etc., until it was time to hit the live pitching. Benny's team had been averaging about 13 strikeouts a game when he started this drill. By the time he finished, they were averaging 2.3 strikeouts per game.

The more you do something, the more it becomes part of you. Benny told me there were three processes of hitting—seeing the ball, thinking, and reacting. Our goal was to eliminate the thinking. I got to the point where I saw the ball and reacted without even thinking. I didn't have to think because I'd done it so many times that I just reacted automatically.

And I'll tell you something else that amazed me about learning to use my hips: It took 10 strokes off my golf game. The first time I went out to play golf that spring I couldn't believe it. I've never been very good with the woods—always pushing the ball off the tee. And I'd never been able to hit a low iron. Now I was amazing myself by dropping balls exactly where I wanted them. Benny laughed when I told him. It's all the same thing, he told me. Same fundamentals, just a different plane.

The problem you have trying to hit live pitching is that you don't have time to think about fundamentals. But through repetition, it can become natural.

Like the time I was with a group of Philadelphia writers at the Cove Restaurant in Wilshire Center in Los Angeles, and I decided to demonstrate hitting. They thought I was out of my mind. We had been talking about hitting, and somebody asked about the fundamentals of hitting off a tee. I said, "I'll show you." So when the valet brought the car around, I opened the trunk and took out my batting tee. I always carry it with me. I put a tennis ball on the tee and whacked it out of sight.

"Now watch this," I told them. "I can do it with my eyes closed."

"No way," said somebody.

"Just watch," I said and whacked two more tennis balls down Seventh Street with my eyes closed. Then I put the tee back into the trunk, and we drove away.

I just can't say enough about what Benny Lefebvre did for me. It must have taken me six weeks that winter to get the new swing down to where it didn't feel awkward. We literally changed everything. It was always "You didn't use your hips," or "No, you let your hands come through," or whatever I was doing wrong. Then one day it just fell into place. Before working with Benny, as you may recall, I had a career batting average of .245.

I've hit .285 since, and during the next five years following the winter of hitting tennis balls, my average was above .300.

Even years later, when I was playing in Philadelphia or Los Angeles, I'd call Benny for reminders. And I was back behind my house during the off-season of 1984–85, before re-signing with the Dodgers, hitting tennis balls off a tee into a net.

I'll tell you something else I always referred to when I went into a slump. It was a letter from Ted Williams.

I wrote him back during the winter of the 1968–69 season. He was managing the Washington Senators then, and I was just a kid he knew very little about. But I wrote and told him how much I respected him as a lifetime .344 hitter and that I was a left-handed hitter, too. Could he give me any advice?

What did I have to lose? I'd been to San Jose three times, El Paso twice, and three times to Seattle. My wife Mary Jayne and I moved six times in one year.

But honestly, I never dreamed Williams would send me a four-page reply, defining his theories on hitting. I've still got the letter and often read it.

The text:

Dear Jay:

There are a few things I think are all-important to anyone, no matter how much ability a fellow has, no matter what style he has, and without ever seeing you. I know this is good solid advice. It is impossible for me to say anything about your swing or how I might help you in this respect, so I am just going to outline what I consider most important in improving anybody's hitting.

When I was a young fellow, back in 1938, I had the great privilege of being acquainted with the greatest right-handed hitter of all times, Rogers Hornsby. He was the only outstanding hitter whom I ever asked, "What do I have to do to be a good hitter?"

Rogers Hornsby said, and after playing professional ball for 25 years myself, I agreed: With all the natural ability and talent in the world, it is impossible to be a really good hitter WITHOUT GETTING A BALL TO HIT! Now, what does that mean?

It means a ball that is not in a tough area for you. It means a ball you are not fooled on, and, of course, I mean this applies only up to two strikes. With two strikes, you simply have to protect the plate. I get a little impatient watching the good hitters today—fellows with great ability—who are not as good as they should be simply because they won't wait for the good pitch to hit.

I've been asked how often I got the ball I was looking for. I would say that it was a good 70 percent of the time.

Certainly, you can't improve without practicing the things you know you are weakest in, and the best place to correct them is during batting practice—CONCEN-TRATED BATTING PRACTICE—not just swinging from your ass. You should analyze what you are doing with every pitch. If you find that you pop up the high pitch, then your thought on the next pitch should be "I have to be quicker," because, as a rule, when you pop up a pitch, your bat has been slow. So you say, "I have to be quicker," and you also have to think about hitting down on the ball. No matter what type of pitch it is, if you haven't hit it solidly, you should immediately think of the correction you have to make.

Whenever I went into a slump, I went back to fundamentals. Wait on the ball, be quick, use a light bat and choke up. I'm an advocate of the light bat, and I'm sure that of all the home runs I hit, at least half of them came when I was choking up slightly.

Just one more thing. Do not try to pull the ball. If you have figured the pitch properly, you are going to get enough pitches that it should be just like batting practice. I'm sure you pull a reasonable amount of balls in practice, so you should never make an effort to do it. It should come naturally.

The point is that anybody is a better hitter when he is not pulling the ball. Take an imaginary swing as if you were trying to pull. You can see that the angle decreases your hitting zone. It becomes a more critical way of meeting the ball solidly.

I certainly wish you a lot of luck and am glad to know that Jimmy Piersall has been helping you.

Sincerely,
Ted Williams

Even though I followed Williams's advice whenever possible—especially about pitch selection—I still needed the mechanical fix that Benny Lefebvre gave me three years later. After seven up-and-down seasons with the Angels and Chisox, I felt I was finally a hitter. I could hardly wait to attack the ball in spring training. But there was one major problem. Nobody wanted me.

Nobody, you see, knew that I was a born-again hitter. I had just hit .188, remember? So Benny Lefebvre was about to get a major assist in the saving of Jay Johnstone's career—and it came from a most unlikely source, Charles O. Finley.

Before Charlie could save me, however, somebody had to dump on me. That man was Stu Holcomb, then general manager of the White Sox. He sent me a contract with a

20-percent pay cut, which I wouldn't accept. I didn't believe that I was the only guy to be blamed for that .188 batting average. All during the previous season the Sox had jacked around with Rick Reichardt in center field ahead of me. I felt that they stuck it to me all season and, frankly, I believe it had to do with my being the player representative and all the problems the players association and owners had in 1972.

But statistics don't lie, right? Holcomb said 20-percent cut. We argued. Finally, he said on the phone, "Why don't you come on down to spring training [at Sarasota] and we'll iron it out. So I flew all night, got to the airport, rented a car, and reported to Holcomb.

"Glad you made it," he said, as he handed me the same contract with the same 20-percent cut, from $25,000 to $20,000.

"What's this? You ask me to fly all night to give me the same contract?"

"That's the best we can do."

"Well, I can't take it."

"We can always trade you."

"Fine, trade me."

"Or we could release you."

"Fine, release me. I'm not signing that contract."

The next day they released not only me but also third baseman Ed Spiezio. They also sent letters to five other guys who were holding out and said, in effect: "The same thing that happened to Johnstone and Spiezio can happen to you." But the other guys—Wilbur Wood was one of them—didn't go for it and eventually got some small raises.

Still, I was out of baseball. I couldn't believe it. I had gotten up at 5:00 A.M. all winter for this? Released. It was worse than being traded. At least when you're traded, there's some place to go. When the White Sox released me, I could only go to the phone.

So I called Charlie Finley, then owner of the Oakland A's. Why Charlie? Because I knew him. We used to hang out at the same restaurant-saloon in Chicago, Tommy O'Leary's, and my wife and I had joined him a few times for dinner.

I distinctly remember the phone conversation:

"Mr. Finley," I said. "I can't find a job."

"Well, Jay, if I were you, I wouldn't put it that way. I'd call and say, 'Mr. Finley, I need a job.' "

"Well, Mr. Finley," I said, "I need a job."

And he gave me one.

He brought me to spring training with his Triple A club, and right away I knew things would work out. I was hitting a ton. I opened the season in Tucson, hit about .360 (final average for 69 games in Tucson was .347), then got called up to Oakland.

This, however, was a great Oakland team. The A's had won the 1972 World Series in seven games over Cincinnati and would go on to win again in 1973 over the Mets. It was a team with Joe Rudi, Reggie Jackson, Sal Bando, Vida Blue, Rollie Fingers, and Catfish Hunter, to name a few. There was really no place for Jay Johnstone, master of hitting tennis balls off a batting tee.

But I was Finley's "up-and-down guy" for the A's that year—back and forth between Tucson and Oakland. I wasn't in the World Series because of Finley's heart attack. He had promised to bring me up with the big club in September, but in late August he was in intensive care, and nobody else would make a decision. I was pretty upset at the time—I remember yelling at the general manager on the phone, "He promised me . . . I don't care if you have to get him out of bed; he promised me." But it didn't happen, and I really had no legitimate complaint. I was only in baseball because Finley liked me, anyhow.

Once he even called me in the dugout during a game. I thought Dick Williams would have a seizure.

This was back when Finley had come up with white

shoes for his players. Fancy uniforms and white shoes. I had just been called up from Tucson, and they had to ship me a pair of white shoes to Kansas City, where we were playing. Now the games in Kansas City start at 7:30 P.M., and I guess Charlie thought they started at 8:00. So we must be at least 20 minutes into the game, late in the first inning, when the phone rang in the dugout. Then I heard Williams say, "Jay, telephone."

"Telephone?"

So I went down and took the phone from my manager, who stood right there next to me, and it was the owner on the other end of the line.

"How do the shoes fit?" Finley asked me.

"Oh, the shoes are fine. Leather's great," I said. "It shouldn't take me long to break them in. Uhhh, we're in the first inning, Mr. Finley."

"Oh," he said, surprised. "Well, I'm glad the shoes fit, and if you have any other problems, just call old Charlie and let me know."

I handed the phone back to Williams, who was probably wondering by then if this new kid had been named the new manager.

Finley was never shy about providing his input. I've seen Williams make lineup changes after getting a phone call from LaPorte, Indiana, where Charlie lived.

Unfortunately, or fortunately—in baseball, we never know—I wasn't destined to remain much longer in Finley's world. Charlie lent me to the St. Louis Cardinals the following spring—one of those $25,000 waiver deals if I made the club. And I killed the ball. I mean I crushed it. A games, B games, whatever. When I wasn't getting two hits, I was getting three.

But just as I was set to go north (they had already told me I had made the club), the Cardinals came up with a pitching problem. They had too many pitchers, and it came down to a choice between Tim McCarver and me. They kept Tim. (Ironically, we later became teammates in Philly.)

So now I belonged to Finley again, but he had one of the best baseball teams in our time—world champions twice in a row.

"We really don't have room for you," Charlie told me. "But I'll make some calls around for you."

And by now, I guess, some other people were beginning to realize that perhaps Jay Johnstone had learned how to hit. The Dodgers called and the Phillies called. Paul Owens of the Phillies got to me first. I spent part or all of the next five seasons in Philadelphia.

But Tom Lasorda wasn't going to get off that easy. His time to be terrorized was coming.

In Philly, I hit .295, .329, .318, and .284 in successive seasons, before being traded during the 1978 season to the Yankees for pitcher Rawly Eastwick. It was not a popular trade with Philly fans. It has since been called one of the worst trades Paul Owens ever made.

It didn't do much for me, either. Not only was I giving up a preferred diet of National League pitching, but there was no room for me within the makeup of the Yankee team. Once I realized it, I asked to be traded again. George Steinbrenner complied (do you think my impending free agency at the end of 1979 had anything to do with it?), and this left-handed hitting Gulliver headed back to California (San Diego Padres), which I hadn't wanted to leave in the first place.

The California (Angels)-to-Chicago-to-California (A's)-to-Philadelphia-to-New York-to-California (Padres) sojourn had taken nine years.

And I still hadn't played for my fourth California team, the Dodgers. Tom Lasorda, the poor soul, still didn't know what he was missing.

During those final two months of the 1979 season, before becoming a free agent, I played almost every day with the Padres and hit .294. It felt good to be back in the National League.

Ironically, the Dodgers signed me as a free agent for 1980 because they wanted a left-handed pinch hitter. But for various reasons I played 109 games and led the team in hitting with .307.

Then came the 1981 strike, the split season, my relegation to being a pinch hitter, and a batting average of .295. Gulliver didn't know it, but it was almost time again to move on.

By now, perhaps you're getting a feel for the ball player's existence. Places and people, people and places—with careers often boosted or broken by the strangest of circumstances.

You've heard about right place, right time? I often think about the first time I got to the big leagues (1966). I had just gotten out of the Marines, but refused to report to Double A (El Paso) because Chuck Tanner and I were at war (that story comes later). Well, you know how many players get away with refusing anything in baseball. I had no choice. I went to El Paso for about 10 days, hit .360 (seven games), and was called up to the Angels' Triple A club in Seattle. I hit .340 there in 81 games and got the call to Anaheim.

But I wouldn't have been in Seattle in the first place if outfielder Al Spangler hadn't had four wisdom teeth pulled on the same day that outfielder Mike White dived for a ball and dislocated his shoulder. They had to have a replacement. Right time, right place.

And despite that .340 batting average in Seattle, the Angels wouldn't have called me up if Rick Reichardt hadn't needed a kidney operation.

It would be accurate to say, then, that I reached the major leagues because of wisdom teeth, a dislocated shoulder, and a kidney operation. What did you want? A homemade bat, a bolt of lightning, and a home run that blew out the lights? Everybody can't be Roy Hobbs. Hell, I would have settled for a hangnail and gallstones if it had gotten me into the big leagues.

Everybody can't always catch a good break, either. They do go the other way. Consider the day I knocked Billy Connors off the Chicago Cubs' roster. It was enough to make a grown pitcher cry.

Connors, now a very respected pitching coach for the Cubs, was a pitcher with the same organization in 1967. It was the final spring-training game of the season, Cubs vs. Angels in Palm Springs, and Connors already had the club made. It figured that one day later he would be going north.

Leo Durocher, however, was managing the Cubs. Nothing was ever a sure thing with Leo. And on this particular day, he had Connors, a right-hander, warming up for five innings in the bullpen. That's enough to wear out anybody, but Connors wasn't going to complain. He just kept getting up and down, waiting for the call.

Finally, in the bottom of the 10th, Durocher called for relief. I'm the hitter. I hit Billy's first pitch over the fence into a parking lot full of vans and RVs. Home run. Game is over, and Leo never liked to lose in Palm Springs because that's where Frank Sinatra lives.

Durocher went into a rage, sent Connors to Escondido, and kept rookie Joe Niekro on the Cubs staff instead. Connors never pitched again for the Cubs, but it was the beginning of a very successful career for Niekro. And I can't remember whether my eyes were open or closed when I hit that home run.

Call it a break of the game. Call it wrong time, wrong place for Billy Connors. Mostly, call it bad luck. Don't ever tell a ball player there is no such thing as luck.

Yet there is one place in baseball where luck is seldom a

factor. That's in the front office. The haul is too long and expensive for poorly managed franchises to succeed. They can only rely so long on luck.

Teams take on the personalities of their owners. Managers may come and go—which they do, inasmuch as they are all members of the same fraternity—but management controls the destiny of a baseball team. If you're going to have a first-class operation, your team will be first class. If you have a Mickey Mouse operation, your team will feature Goofy and Pluto. It's that simple.

It is no mystery why successful teams repeat success. The Dodgers, for example, go first class—accommodations for players, equipment, instructors, staff, public relations, you name it. And look at the Dodgers' record of success since moving to Los Angeles.

Look, too, at the change in the Cubs. New ownership (The Tribune Company) decided to spend some money, and what happened? They had a winner for the first time since the end of World War II. And look at what happened in Minnesota. They finally got a new ballpark and spent some money. And they almost won their division title in 1984.

Detroit's Tigers, with new ownership, won the world championship in 1984. They beat the San Diego Padres, who had gotten aggressive at the free-agent marketplace and acquired such established stars as Steve Garvey, Graig Nettles, and Goose Gossage. And after San Diego pitching failed so miserably in the 1984 World Series, what did the Padres do? They made an off-season trade for LaMarr Hoyt.

If you want to know about a team's morale, call me. But don't call collect or wait too long. I might not be there anymore.

❝

George Steinbrenner came up with one of the most ingenious curfew checks when I was with the Yankees. He gave the security guard a baseball and told him to get the autograph of any player who came in after midnight.

❞

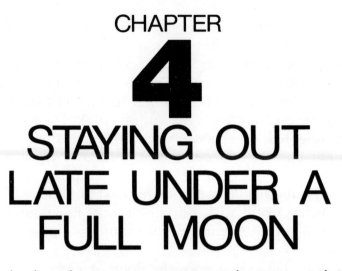

CHAPTER
4
STAYING OUT LATE UNDER A FULL MOON

"I plead guilty to assigning Jay Johnstone and Jim Piersall as roommates. It was an easy decision. I didn't want to screw up two rooms."

Bill Rigney

It was while I was playing for my third major league team that somebody asked manager Bill Rigney, "How did Johnstone end up in Oakland?" Rig answered, "Neil Armstrong brought him back from the moon."

One year, during spring training with the Angels, Jimmy Piersall said to a reporter, "You think I'm goofy? Then I wish to tell you that Jay Johnstone is a real moon man. He gets up every morning and shines his shoes before he brushes his teeth, and he's washed that car [a 1967 Thunderbird] every day. That car has a stereo he plays night and day. Some people sit in their room and listen to music. No. We have to sit in the car."

It was 1985, during spring training with the Expos, when manager Bob Rogers said to a reporter, "I'll tell you how Jay Johnstone got his nickname. One day he lost a ball in the sun, but when he came back to the bench he said, 'I lost it in the moon.' After that we called him 'Moon Man.' "

My purpose is not to dispute the comments from any of

the above-mentioned gentlemen. But I do have a different version of how I got that nickname.

It was spring training, 1967, with the Angels in Palm Springs, and my roomie was Fred Newman, a right-hander physically but a guy who thought like a left-hander. And, as was the custom, we went out one night for a drink.

But one led to several, and the next thing I knew midnight curfew had come and gone and we were still sitting in the saloon. We definitely had a problem.

Now it's about 1:00 A.M., and we coast into the rear of the Gene Autry Hotel with our lights out. Fortunately, our room was in the rear and we quietly tiptoed to the entrance.

"Be quiet when you open the door," I said.

"I don't have a key. You open it."

"I don't have a key either."

So there we stand—reeling a little, wondering if hotel security is going to come cruising past.

"Go to the lobby and get a key," he said.

"And get caught for breaking curfew? Are you nuts? You go to the lobby and get a key."

To be truthful, neither of us could afford to get caught; Newman was on thin ice trying to make the pitching staff, and I was just a rookie. So we stood there a little longer.

"Let's sleep in the car," he said, finally.

"No, let me try to jimmy the window first," I said.

So I'm jiggling and moving and shaking the window and Newman, who stood about 6'5", was standing right over me. Finally I said, "Freddy, will you please back the fuck away and let the moon shine in so I can see?"

"That's all you need," said Newman, "More moonshine."

Well, luck prevailed, I got the window open, and the story went through the clubhouse pretty quickly the next day: Rookie saves veteran from sleeping in the car. And that's when Fregosi started calling me "Moon Man."

Next thing I knew the manager, Rigney, picked up on it, and instead of "Hey, kid," or "Hey, No. 10" it was now

"Hey, Moon"—and when I walked into the clubhouse, teammates even sang "Moonlight Becomes You," and "Shine On Harvest Moon."

Moon: A celestial body revolving around the earth from west to east in a lunar month of 29.3 days.

To Moon: Exposing the posterior portions of terrestrial body or bodies, with intent to shock, entertain, and embarrass.

I once mooned Merv Griffin. It was no big deal, but at the time it seemed like the thing to do.

It was prior to an appearance on "The Merv Griffin Show" by the Big Blue Wrecking Crew—singers Steve Yeager, Rick Monday, Jerry Reuss, and me—following the Dodgers' 1981 World Series triumph. We had recorded this song, "We Are the Champions," as a giggle more than anything, with any proceeds going to charity.

So we were practicing onstage before we were to perform live. People were already beginning to take their seats. During a break, I climbed up to the catwalk with the spotlights. And just as people downstairs were starting to look for me, they heard, "Oh, Merv!" and everybody looked up.

He said it was the only time he'd ever been mooned in his own studio.

I don't know why ball players like to moon. Maybe it's the only way some of them can figure out how to express themselves.

Once Reuss and I mooned the entire Cincinnati Reds' bench. Don Stanhouse had commandeered a groundskeepers' cart, and it was just before batting practice, so almost all of the Reds were sitting in their dugout.

Stan the Man Unusual makes a sweep past the dugout, and we're standing in the back of the cart, hanging a double moon on them.

Mooning, however, is hardly confined to ball players.

The Dodgers found that out during a spring bus trip from Vero Beach to Fort Lauderdale. A couple of girls drove past, and, sure enough, somebody in the back of the bus hung a moon for them. Big laugh, right?

Well, a few miles down the road they reciprocated. They pulled right in front of the bus and mooned the entire team out of the back window of the car. Lasorda sits in the front seat, so he got the full shot. He couldn't believe his eyes.

"Follow that car . . . follow that car," he yelled, with the entire bus breaking up.

Sometimes a moon can be good therapy—something outrageous and off-the-wall to take a person's mind off depressing things.

The Dodgers were in Atlanta, for example, and Lasorda was really down in the dumps after we lost a tough game. I mean Dracula has nothing on Tom Lasorda when he's depressed. He'll walk the streets for hours. That's how much he hates to lose.

It was late, and Reuss, Garvey, and I walked into this restaurant. We saw Lasorda sitting over by the bar with traveling secretary Billy De Lury. Just the two of them, and nobody was talking. So we invited them to join us, but Tommy refused. He said he wanted to be alone.

So while Garv and Reuss held his attention, talking across the room, I slipped out and came back through the rear door of the kitchen. Then I stood on a stool inside the swinging kitchen door and yelled, "Tom, Tom, Tom!"

"Whattaya want?"

"Somebody wants to take your picture."

He didn't want to turn, but he couldn't stop himself. I wasn't more than 10 feet away, standing on this stool with the door now open, hanging a moon.

He just couldn't keep a straight face. Here was a man really trying to be upset, and he couldn't. After that, he joined us.

Much of a ball player's waking hours are spent late at night. Because of night games, we have become nocturnal animals—meals at 1:00 A.M., sleeping until noon, to the ball park for whirlpool or early hitting at 3:00 P.M., regular bus at 4:45 P.M., and so on. In reality, there is no longer such a thing as a curfew.

It wasn't always that way, especially in spring training. I can remember when Angels' manager Lefty Phillips would sit up half the night in the lobby, watching for players.

Players knew in those days that if you stayed out late, you stayed out all night. That way you wouldn't get caught. Why come in at 12:30 A.M. and get fined when you could come in at 8:00 A.M. and be safe?

We knew Lefty wouldn't be calling rooms after midnight because of Fregosi, the team leader and my pal and ex-business partner (we once tried the pearl-importing business). Why? Because one night a coach called Fregosi's room, and he started screaming, "If you ever call my fuckin' room again, I'll choke your fuckin' head off . . . I'm tryin' to get my rest and you're wakin' me up over this fuckin' curfew . . . what kind of a team is this?"

Actually, I think Jim wanted everybody to think he had a girl in the room at the time, but isn't offense always the best defense? They never called rooms anymore, and guys could start staying out all night if they wished.

But you were always taking a chance. A couple of players were caught one night coming into the hotel with women on their arms. And Dick Miller, an LA sportswriter who commanded absolutely no respect from the players, ran their names in headlines the next day, rather than protect them. One player, Rudy May, always felt the incident precipitated his divorce.

Have you ever heard the curfew story about Sandy Koufax and the lost diamond? Larry Sherry tells it best:

"It was spring training in Vero Beach, early 1960s, and we had rigid curfew. But Sandy and I had been working hard and were ready to break out. So we go down to Port St. Lucie for some pizza and beer. But we stay too late, and now we know we've got a problem. We were staying in those old barracks then in Dodgertown, and it was tough to sneak in, especially if the old man [Walter Alston] was awake.

"Well, he was up that night because Stan Williams had come in late from playing poker and got chewed out. Our problem was that Walter also looked into Stan's room and saw that his roommate, Sandy, still wasn't home. So he waits up for him.

"So here we come, trying to slip in, and we hear Alston yelling, 'Is that you, Koufax?' Right away, he's got Sandy pinned against the wall, chewing him out—but I scoot on down to my room and lock the door. My roommate is Johnny Podres.

"It doesn't work. Here comes Alston after me, and he's livid. I'm so scared I won't unlock the door. I'm sitting in there on my bed, and he's outside pounding and yelling, 'I know it's you, Sherry, I know it's you.'

"We both catch hell, of course, and we both get fined. But the kicker was that Walter lost the diamond out of his 1959 World Series ring when he was pounding on my door. He never did find it.

"And from then on, Koufax would yell at me, 'Hey, Larry, have you checked your door for diamonds lately?' "

George Steinbrenner came up with one of the most ingenious curfew checks when I was with the Yankees.

He had all of the players rooming on the second floor of his hotel in Tampa when we would play exhibition games in that area of Florida. And he stationed a guard by the elevator door in the hallway to enforce midnight curfew.

The cute part was this: He gave the guard a baseball and

told him to get the autograph of any player who came in after midnight. So, when a player got out of the elevator, this sweet little old man would say, "Would you please autograph my baseball?"

It was very sneaky. About eight guys signed the ball, and there were their names for Steinbrenner to see the next morning. Unfortunately, three of the names were rookies, and George got so mad he immediately sent them back to the minors to set an example for the rest of us.

Reggie Jackson, Thurman Munson, and I also came in late, but I escaped signing the ball because I came up the back stairs instead of using the elevator. My room was at the end of the hall near the stairs. The guard didn't see me because there was a Coke machine obscuring the door to my room. Reggie and Thurman got fined.

That happened on the first night we stayed at the hotel. We then had to make adjustments. And on the day we were to check out, the hotel manager went to Steinbrenner and pointed out that he had found a couple of bed sheets tied together and thrown over the outside balcony.

"If my players are smart enough to do that, then they deserve to get away with it," said George, and I always admired him for that.

I suppose that missing curfew should be my forte, given my reputation for executing spectacular disappearing acts. Tom Lasorda says that I'm the only player he knows who should have a beeper. I guess I do have a tendency to disappear.

I'm a wanderer. I don't need a reason. I just take off.

I simply can't stand sitting still. Like in a game. If I'm not playing, I can't just sit there and watch. I might go through the runway to hit into the batting cage or maybe sit at the end of the dugout to look into the stands for pretty girls. Anything to keep from getting bored.

If I still didn't consider myself a player, maybe it would be a different story. I guess I can understand how those designated hitters in the American League have gotten their brains into sort of a no-man's land—just sitting there with a bat between your legs and waiting your turn. But I've always considered myself a player, and I can't sit for nine innings and watch a baseball game.

I'm the same way when I'm home. My wife will be talking to me, turn her head for a split second, and I'll be gone. She tried to explain to me that I had the attention span of a three-year-old, but I didn't listen long enough to understand what she was saying.

During a conversation I'm different. I could sit still all day long and discuss politics or religion. I love to argue. I don't even care which side of the issue I take. Frankly, it's a good way to find out about the personality of the other person.

But if I'm watching a John Wayne movie on television and somebody is trying to talk to me, he or she might as well be talking to the wall. Once I focus on the TV, you can't get me away.

There was a time, before he understood me, that Lasorda would get very aggravated when he couldn't find me. Like the time he said to me, "I might want you to hit. Go loosen up."

So I go back into the runway next to the Dodger locker room and start running. Then he changed his mind and wanted me to hit right away. But he couldn't find me. I was running.

Then he was pissed and screaming, "Where the hell were you when I needed you to hit?"

"I was getting loose like you told me," I said.

Finally I figured out the way to handle his complaints about my absence. At the beginning of a game I would go sit right next to him, right there with the coaches, and I'd talk to him. I'd bother him, harass him a little—ask him if he wanted coffee or tea—until finally he'd yell, "Get the hell out of here!"

Then I could go do whatever I wanted for the rest of the

game. I might go for coffee or maybe go into my Monty Hall routines. The coaches might want some peanuts, for example, so I'd grab a baseball, step outside the dugout, and yell, "Anybody want to trade two bags of peanuts for a baseball?"

John Vukovich, a coach for the Cubs, would get down-right exasperated when he couldn't find me.

"Jay," he would shout, "I know you work hard, but you can't go through life working just on your own schedule. When we're supposed to hit, you're supposed to hit. Is that so hard to understand?"

John had been irritated because that day in spring training in Mesa, Arizona, I had been absent from my turn in the batting cage. He had looked everywhere—the john, training room, locker room, everywhere.

Finally, just as he was about to give up, somebody came through the clubhouse door, and Vuke saw a flash of my uniform—just the rear end, actually—outside in the parking lot. One of our players' wives, Mrs. Warren Brusstar, was having car trouble, and I was inside the hood trying to help her.

I don't understand why Vuke got so upset. I'd want somebody to help my wife if she had car trouble.

Monty Basgall bears the brunt of my wandering with the Dodgers, although I did have some fun with another coach, Ron Perranoski, during 1985 spring training. One of the sportswriters was looking for me, and I heard him ask Perranoski, "Where's Johnstone?"

"You're asking me?" said Perranoski.

"Well, you've got the clipboard with the workout sched-ule," said the writer. "It's 11:15 A.M., so where is Jay?"

"I can only tell you where he's supposed to be," said Perry, looking at his clipboard. "He's supposed to be on field number one."

I had been in the john listening, and just as Perranoski

mentioned where I was supposed to be, I wandered past both of them without even saying hello. And as I headed for the clubhouse door with my bat, I saw Perry throw up his arms and say, "See?"

Danny Ozark, manager of the Phillies, probably had more trouble keeping track of me than anyone. It became an obsession with him. He kept looking for me at a certain time and could never understand where I was. Then one day he found me in the equipment room doing a radio show.

"What's the big deal?" I asked him. "I'm out here at the same time every day."

One other time Danny was looking for me during a game—something about pinch hitting, I think—and found me in his office with my feet on his desk, making a phone call. I wasn't trying to act like a manager. It was the only phone with a direct outside line.

Before Lasorda, Ozark was my favorite target. Once when we were playing the San Francisco Giants, I talked Chris Speier of the Giants into changing into a Phillies uniform and coming into our clubhouse, just to see if Ozark would recognize him. For a minute there, Danny thought we had a new player. Then he recognized Speier and chased him out.

I pinned a picture of smiling Danny in my locker. Written on it was "Dear Jay, Best of Luck. Don't worry about all the rules. They're for the other guys."

I was Ozark's scapegoat, but we had an understanding. He would basically let me do anything I wanted to do, but I also had to be his whipping boy. Whenever he needed to yell at someone, he'd yell at me. It was a good system because he could yell at me to get his point across to everybody, and he knew damned well that I wasn't taking it personally. Most of the time I wasn't even listening.

Once he chewed me out for 10 minutes, and I wasn't even in the room. It was priceless.

He had called an early meeting to discuss our lackadaisical play, and consequently the bus left the hotel 15 minutes earlier than listed on the itinerary. Well, I missed the bus and had to take a taxi.

But the meeting started before I got to the ballpark, and from all reports, it was a doozie. Ozark was chewing guys out right and left—about bad throws from the outfield, sloppy play, lack of hustle, lack of execution, everything he could think of.

Then he started in on me, and as he's yelling he's looking for me. Now the Houston visiting clubhouse is huge, and as Danny is walking up and down, the guys could tell he was searching for my face. He couldn't find it, but that didn't stop him from chewing on me.

Finally, he lets me have a final roast, stalks into his office, and slams the door. Just then, I walk into the clubhouse. Everybody broke up. They told me I'd just gotten my ass chewed out for 10 minutes.

"Well, I'm glad I missed it, then," I said and went into Danny's office to say hello.

It seems I was always in trouble with Danny. In fact, when I got traded to the Yankees, a newspaper cartoon ran the headline. "Out of the Doghouse, Into the Madhouse."

I liked Danny Ozark then and I like him now. He's a scout now with the Giants, and not too long ago we had him over for dinner. He said he was surprised to find me at the table. He thought for sure I would have wandered off.

To be honest, I wasn't sure which way to wander during the winter of 1984–85.

For the first time since 1972, I had no idea what my spring training address would be or, for that matter, if there would even be one.

But the Dodgers needed left-handed hitting from the bench, and once again, Vero Beach became my destination.

This spring training, too, was a little different from all

the others—reminiscent of Holtville, Palm Springs, Sarasota, Clearwater, Fort Lauderdale, and Mesa in routine, perhaps, but special in other ways.

Maybe I was finally beginning to realize, after 22 springs as a baseball professional, that this might be my last as a player.

Or perhaps the stories I heard made it different. Perhaps they brought home to me just how much fun it can be making a living the way we do.

"Hey, I'm writing a silly book," I'd say to some of my friends, "Got any crazy stories you want to tell?"

There were some beauts and believe-it-or-nots, and one of the best came from Ben Wade, director of scouting for the Dodgers. He tells about the strangest play he ever witnessed—four runs scoring in the bottom of the ninth on a two-out ground ball back to the pitcher. The details:

The Dodgers' Tri-Cities farm club was playing in 1966 in Eugene, Oregon, and Duke Snider was manager. Tri-Cities was leading, 4–1, with Eugene at bat, bases loaded, two out, bottom of the ninth.

And inasmuch as it was a long ride back to Tri-Cities, manager Snider already had the bats in his arms, ready to pack. Al Choate was pitching, and the ball was hit right back to him on two easy hops. One toss to first and the game is over.

Instead, all hell broke loose. Let me count the ways:

- Choate's lob to first base sails over Steve Hockensmith's head. One run scores as Hockensmith chases down the ball, hoping to keep the runner on second from scoring.
- Hockensmith picks up the ball and throws it over catcher Ted Sizemore's head as the second run scores.
- Sizemore chases the ball to the backstop screen, turns, and throws down to second, trying to nail the guy who hit the ball back to the pitcher in the first place.

- Sizemore's throw sails over second baseman Billy Grabarkewitz's head and goes into center field, allowing a third run to score.
- Centerfielder Terry Heizenrader runs in, fumbles and kicks the ball, then throws toward home.
- Heizenrader's throw goes over catcher Sizemore's head, the man who hit the two-hopper back to the pitcher scores the winning run, and Duke Snider tosses the bats straight into the air.

Five errors had allowed four runs to score on a ball hit back to the pitcher. Score it Choate-over-Hockensmith-over-Sizemore-over-Grabarkewitz-to-Heizenrader-over-Sizemore.

Can you top that? I can't. But I do like this tale of quick thinking from Dodger minor league pitching instructor Larry Sherry:

Manager Bobby Bragan took his 1958 Spokane Indians into Phoenix for a six-game series. The Phoenix Giants had a powerful team—Willie McCovey, Tom Haller, Andre Rodgers, Dusty Rhodes, Joey Amalfitano, etc.—and they played in a small park. Temperature was 108 degrees. Spokane got murdered in the first two games—scores like 19–4 and 21–6—and everybody was complaining about the heat.

So Bragan calls a clubhouse meeting and screams, "I'm sick and tired of hearing you guys complain about the heat. The next guy who says it's too hot is gonna get fined $50."

It's even hotter the next night as Art Fowler goes to the mound for Spokane. By the third inning his uniform is soaked, his face is beet-red, and he's sitting in the dugout with an ammonia rag over his head. And just as Bragan starts up the dugout steps, Fowler—who doesn't see him—moans, "Gawd, it's hot out here."

Then, seeing Bragan, he whips the rag off his face without missing a beat and says, "Just the way I like it, Bobby."

Dodger scout Rafael Avila swears this one is true:

It was Rafael Landestoy's first game as a professional, 1973, with the Licey club in the Dominican Republic. Avila was a coach and instructed Landestoy to go into the outfield for defense in the late innings.

Somebody ripped a line drive along the foul line to the gravel warning track, and as Landestoy reached for the ball he looked back at the runner. Then he dropped the ball and had to reach again.

Unknowingly, this time he came up with an orange, which he relayed to shortstop Bobby Valentine, who looked into his glove and said, "What in hell do I do with this?"

Red Adams, former major league pitching coach in Los Angeles, tells this one on himself:

"I went to the mound to settle down Happy [Burt Hooton]. The bases were loaded. I don't remember what I said, but just as I got back to the dugout, the next guy hit a grand slam homer.

"A few innings later Hooton was out of the game and sitting at the end of the dugout with ice on his arm. Now the Montreal pitcher gets into a jam, and their pitching coach goes out.

"And just as he reaches the mound, Hooton cups his hands over his mouth and shouts, 'Tell him the same thing Adams told me!' "

Ted Sizemore offers this anecdote about the power of positive thinking:

It was 1969, Ted's rookie season with the Dodgers, and they were playing in Wrigley Field against the Cubs.

Sizemore reached first base on a hit and, during a pitching change, found himself in a strange conversation with first baseman Ernie Banks.

"You a pretty good hitter?" asked Banks.

"Uhh, I'm OK, I guess," said the frightened rookie.

"That's not right," yelled Banks, "You're the best hitter in the world, right? You got to believe that, Ted Sizemore. You're the best hitter in the world."

"Well, I'm going to be a major league hitter, I'll tell you that," said Sizemore, working up some courage.

"No, no, no," said Banks, "You're the best. The best. Say it. Say that you're the best hitter in the world!"

Exasperated and a little embarrassed, Sizemore finally thought, "The hell with it," and started yelling, "I'm the best hitter in the world, I'm the best hitter in the world."

"No, you're not," smiled Banks. "You're the second best. I'm the best."

"

Once, after Bill Russell made four errors in an exhibition game, I went out early the next day, roped off the seats behind first base, and placed sandbags in front of the fence. Then I put up a sign that read: "Enter at your own risk. Bill Russell is playing shortstop today. All seats 25 cents."

"

CHAPTER
5
MR. PRESIDENT
AND THE
BAD BOYS

"He gave me a chocolate hand by putting a brownie in my glove, then he gave me a stained head by putting chewing tobacco in my batting helmet. But what can I say? He's my friend."

Steve Garvey

When Steve Garvey becomes President of the United States, I would like to become Secretary of Defense. Minister of Pranks and Pratfalls? Undersecretary of Gags and Giggles? Surely there will be a place for me in Garv's cabinet.

He *will* run for public office. He has been for years. I know I'll vote for him, and I'll tell why: What you see is what you get. Steve Garvey is the same person off the field as on, the same away from the interview or camera as with it. He is not a phony. He does not present one person in public and another in private.

He really is Goody Two-Shoes, Butter-in-the-Mouth, Apple Pie, American Flag, and Chevrolet.

For laughs, he goes out and buys a hat and does impersonations of Tom Landry.

It's so sickening that you have to like the guy. I've never known a more sincere, principled man. Underneath, though, I suspect he's a little like Jerry Reuss or myself. It

71

must be the Irish in him. Garv swears that his ancestors' name was O'Garvey and the O was dropped so somebody could move up in the alphabetical order line at Ellis Island.

Reuss and I spent one entire spring training trying to get Garvey to say "fuck." He just wouldn't do it. It's not part of his vocabulary. But we nagged and nagged and nagged until, finally, he turned on us and shouted, "Fuck, fuck, fuck, fuck, fuck, fuck, fuck, fuck, fuck, fuck. See, I said it. Fuck, fuck, fuck, fuck."

But we never could get him to say "motherfucker."

The only thing that worries me about Garvey becoming a U.S. senator or president is his hair. How is he going to walk down that stairway from a jet without a ball cap to keep his hair in place? His hair isn't styled; it's carved.

We were in Atlanta with the Dodgers, back in 1981, and Garv called me in my hotel room.

"Let's go down to the pool and read the papers," he said.

So we go to the pool. Then he says, "Have you eaten?"

"How could I eat? I came to the pool with you."

Now we read the papers a little longer, and he says, "Let's go to lunch."

"OK, let's eat in the hotel," I said, knowing that Garv hates to eat in hotels. On the other hand, I didn't want to be traipsing all over Atlanta looking for lunch.

"Aaahhh, I know this great place for frozen yogurt," he said. "They put strawberries in it and blueberries and all those good things."

So I agreed. Now we go back to our rooms to get ready. Twenty minutes later my phone rings.

"What are you doing?" he said.

"What do you mean, what am I doing? I'm getting ready."

"Well," he said, and there was a long pause.

"Garv, what's on your mind?"

"Well, I. . . ."

"Garv, you can tell me, I'm your friend, remember?"

"Well, I took a shower, and uhhh, I forgot my hair dryer. Do you have a hair dryer?"

He could not say it. He wanted to borrow my hair dryer.

"Yeah, Garv, I've got a hair dryer. Do you want to use it?"

"I'll be right down."

Then we went traipsing around Atlanta looking for frozen yogurt with strawberries and blueberries.

Steve Garvey is very neat. His clothes are always clean, his face washed, his shoes shined, his off-the-field wardrobe impeccable. He honors his father and mother. He is an executive with a company pledged to helping professional athletes find careers after sports. When he comes into a hotel lobby to meet special friends, he always brings a single rose for each lady. At restaurants, he sits at table number one. He wears Top-Siders, ties his sweater over his shoulders just so, never rejects an autograph seeker, is always fashionably late, scrawls personal notes, shaves with a chisel and a hammer, and would never, ever pick his nose.

You gotta burn a guy like that. So I got Garv by melting brownies in his first baseman's mitt.

We were in San Francisco for a day game, and, believe it or not, the weather was hot. Some young girls, Dodgers fans, had baked brownies and sent them to our dugout. Already though, they were getting gooey. So I took the messiest one I could find and stuck it to the infield ball like a giant piece of gum. Then I put the ball and the brownie into the pocket of Garvey's glove.

Garv is very peculiar about his glove, shoes, cap, and bat. I know this. So now I take some of the chocolate stuff from my fingers and rub it onto the side of Reuss's pants without his knowing it. Now the game is about to start, and I sprint across the field toward the clubhouse. As I pass first base umpire Paul Runge, I say, "Paul, watch when Garv comes out." Then I keep going toward the clubhouse door in the right-field corner, and I tell the Giants in their dugout, "Watch Garv."

Garv pops out for the final out of our half-inning, runs into the dugout just like always, grabs his glove and sunglasses, and runs to his position at first base. Now he puts his glove under his arm while he adjusts his glasses.

Then he puts on the glove and reaches in for the ball. Suddenly he just drops it as if it's radioactive. He drops the glove, ball, everything. And he's got chocolate all over his hands. He can't get the stuff out of the glove, and he's got nowhere to wipe it because he doesn't want to get his uniform messy.

Finally he turns to Runge, calls "time out" and runs across into the Dodger dugout to get a towel.

"Who's been screwing around with my glove?"

Nobody answers. I'm not even there. I'm watching from the clubhouse door in foul territory.

At the end of the inning, he comes running into the dugout, and what's the first thing he sees? He sees chocolate on the pants of Reuss. He runs right over, jumps on Jerry's lap, and starts thumping him on the chest. Reuss is dumbfounded. He doesn't even know he has chocolate on his pants.

"Don't ever fool with my glove again," Garv is yelling, and Reuss is trying to protect himself.

This is the first time I've ever admitted to Garv that I was the culprit. I hope it doesn't cost me the Secretary of Defense job.

Garv, however, is always going to need someone to share lunch with him. To many baseball players, lunch has become a ritual—an interlude from the ballpark-to-hotel-to-ballpark-for-another-night-game tedium of a long season. Garv loves his lunches on the road.

Once he called in Cincinnati and suggested lunch. I said OK and told him I'd meet him in the hotel coffee shop.

"Nah, you know I don't like to eat in the hotel. I've got a special place. Best buffet you'll ever eat."

"Where is it?"

"Surprise," Garv said, "Meet me in the lobby in fifteen minutes."

He was late, as usual, and as we left the lobby I started for a taxi.

"Oh, no," said Garv, "We can walk. It builds the appetite."

So we walked. First two blocks this way, then three blocks the other way, then two more blocks, and finally we came to this old building. He pushed the elevator button to the third floor, and I was thinking to myself "Boy, this must be some exclusive joint."

"Just trust me," said Garv, with that sly grin. "Greatest buffet you'll ever eat in your life."

It was the Playboy Club. I couldn't believe it. There were girls all over the place with their boobs hanging out, and Garv brought me there for the buffet. He didn't even notice the girls, and I could hardly drink my coffee. This man is amazing.

He is also a dessert freak. Once Mike Corey, Garv's business partner in PACE, the career development company for athletes, told a waiter at Ambria, a very expensive Chicago restaurant, that Garv was writing a book on desserts. We had 12 in the party. The next thing we knew they brought out 35 different kinds of desserts for "Mr. Garvey and his party" to sample.

Once Reuss, Don Stanhouse, and I tried to "pants" Garv in the outfield, but he's so damned muscular we couldn't get them down. Besides, we all started laughing—Garv had both me and Reuss in a headlock—and the more we laughed, the more impossible the task became.

Garv had his own methods of revenge. Once when Reuss was pitching, he had nothing. The first six guys hit line drives against him. The catcher had hardly touched the ball. Finally, with a man on first, Reuss glanced over toward Garvey, who was holding the runner on first base.

"Waste one," said Garvey.

When the Dodgers lost Garv in the fall of 1982 to free agency and the San Diego Padres (he came within an inch of signing with the Cubs—how would that have changed the outcome of the 1984 NL playoffs?), they lost more than an enduring, power-hitting, slick-fielding first baseman. They lost one of baseball's class acts.

It's funny, though, how certain people don't get along. I like Ron Cey. I like Steve Garvey. Ron Cey and Steve Garvey have never been friends. That doesn't mean they didn't play well together and communicate when they were Dodgers. They just didn't pal together. Every team has situations like that.

Ironically, Garv and the Penguin lived in the same neighborhood when they played for the Dodgers, and one day they both had to share a ride into Dodger Stadium with Bill Buckner and one of his friends. Now Bucky never talks in the mornings, anyhow—I know because I lockered next to him in Chicago—and he and Garv weren't exactly pals, either. So here were these three guys, all teammates, in a car together, and there is no conversation.

"Strangest ride of my life," said Buckner's friend afterward. "For 45 minutes nobody said a word. After a while, I started talking to the steering wheel."

So what's unusual about that? I'd rather talk to the steering wheel than be a toilet-beater like Larry Bowa, a.k.a. the Tasmanian Devil.

I played on two teams with Bowa, the Phillies in the '70s and Cubs in the '80s, and although he is a friend, I probably should have reported him long ago as a shameful, degenerate, abusive toilet-beater. Maybe he could have gone somewhere for help.

It was 1977, back when I was playing more often with the Phillies and popping with some power (15 HRs, 59 RBIs), that I first witnessed Bowa's bowl-bashing routine. He had just taken a called third strike and was enraged at the umpire. But while he was screaming at the ump he startéd hitting the toilet bowl with his bat. Then he beat the partition. Caved it in actually. By the time he finished, all that remained was the bowl, and it was so smashed it looked like Jaws, with water running out all over the place.

When the owner, Ruly Carpenter, heard about the toilet damage, he was enraged. He figured somebody should pay. But when he came into the clubhouse to investigate, the first player he ran into was Bowa.

"Jay Johnstone got mad and did it," said Bowa, when Carpenter saw the damage. "I tried to stop him, but you know Jay. He was a crazy man."

So I get fined $750. It came out of my paycheck, and right away my wife was all over me. "What in the hell is this $750 for breaking a toilet?" said Mary Jayne. "Have you flipped out altogether?"

It took me a couple of months to convince Carpenter I was innocent and get my money back.

When I joined Bowa with the Cubs in 1982, I stayed at his house before getting settled. The guy drove me nuts because all he thought or talked about was baseball. We'd go to the park early, like maybe 8:00 A.M. and nobody else would get there until 9:00 or 10:00. Then after the games we'd go for dinner, then go home and watch the White Sox on cable TV. We did this for about 10 days and finally I said, "Larry, have you ever heard of 'Hill Street Blues' or 'Magnum P.I.'?"

The Cubs were losing, then, however, and Larry wasn't hitting. He was struggling so badly, in fact, that he took his bat after another toilet. He beat it down until there was nothing left. Porcelain was flying everywhere. Finally, having seen this act before, I stuck my head around the corner and said, "Hey, Larry, those are the best swings you've had since I've been here."

He threw his helmet at me and missed.

I've known a lot of ball players—hundreds, thousands?—but Bowa flips out worse than any I've ever seen. He just freaks out. But give me a team of Larry Bowas and I'll win a pennant every year.

Once he was called out on a half-swing by Bruce Froemming, who was umping at first base, and Larry started screaming at him after getting back to the dugout. Well, Froemming takes no guff. He gave Larry the thumb, and something snapped.

Bowa ran out of the dugout straight for Froemming, but Ray Ripplemeyer, our pitching coach, grabbed him from behind. Now Rip is a big guy who played college basketball. Bowa is 5'10", 155. But he flipped Ripplemeyer right over his back and kept right on going after Froemming.

Now I was out of the dugout on a dead run, and I tackled Bowa from behind. I held his legs just long enough for Greg Luzinski, "The Bull," to fall on top of him. It was the only way we could have stopped him.

Another of baseball's great red-asses is Lou Piniella of the Yankees. He's also one of the great guys to be around. But when Lou gets upset, he gets physically upset.

When Piniella fired his helmet into the corner of the Yankee dugout, players would scatter like tenpins. Once he got so mad that he went screaming all the way up the runway, across the corridor, through the clubhouse, and into the eating area. Then he jumped and spiked the pictures on the wall. Two days later he jumped up and spiked our coffeepot—put a hole in it about two inches above the bottom—and when the guys came in the next morning for a day game and found no coffee, Lou-Lou really caught hell.

Lou likes to kick, and when he's mad he starts looking

for a water fountain. Bowa hates toilets. Piniella hates water fountains. Everybody to his own taste.

At Yankee Stadium, Lou always had his standby water fountain at the end of the dugout to kick, but on the road he gets confused. In Detroit once, he couldn't find a water fountain, so he attacked a jug-dispenser of Gatorade on the top step. And just as he kicked it, big Cliff Johnson started to walk up the dugout steps. It went all over his uniform and down into his shoes and socks.

Cliff Johnson, 6'4", 230, is not someone who likes Gatorade in his socks. But Piniella escaped alive.

On the other hand, Rich (Goose) Gossage, 6'3" and 225, is not one to have his head banged into a wall. And Chris Chambliss, 6'1" and 225, may never again feel safe when he goes to the john. The three of them—Johnson, Gossage, and Chambliss—were principal characters in the baseball fight I most enjoyed watching. I had an orchestra seat: sitting in the sauna of the Yankee Stadium clubhouse.

This was 1978, and the fight between Cliff and Goose made major headlines because Gossage ended up on the disabled list. What didn't get a lot of attention was how Chambliss got caught in the middle with his pants down.

It all started with guys jawing back and forth over who could hit what. Cliff was having trouble then, and somebody says, "Maybe you could hit a basketball if somebody threw it up there."

"I could hit a fastball if someone would ever throw one," shoots back Johnson, who had been seeing nothing but breaking pitches.

"If I threw a fastball," says Gossage, "all you'd do is hear it."

Now Goose walks into the urinal to take a leak, and as he's standing there, Cliff walks past and says, "Aw, Goose, I could hit your fastball, too." But as he says it, he playfully whacks Goose with those humongous hands, and the force of the slap bangs Goose's head against the wall.

Now Goose, reasonably unhappy, elbows Cliff on the side of his chest, and Goose is pissing on the wall. So they start shoving and arguing.

I'm watching all of this from the sauna with Thurman Munson. We're looking right at them, a couple of bull moose in underwear and socks. And we also have a unique view of Chambliss, who's sitting on the stool in one of those partitioned toilets. Actually, all we can see is his feet and ankles, with his pants down around them.

So the fight starts, and we come out of the sauna to see what we can do. Other guys come also—there must have been six or seven of us—and poor little Brian Doyle jumps in between them. The next thing he knows is that some of those swings are falling short and landing on top of his head.

Finally we get them apart, but they're screaming and cussing, and before anybody can stop it, they're fighting again. Somebody says, "Oh, hell, just let 'em fight," and we step back.

Now they're in a clinch and banging against this toilet partition, and the wall starts caving in on Chambliss.

"What's going on out there?" he's squeaking, in his real high voice, and all you can see is his feet coming up and down off the floor.

Now somebody takes another swing, and the partition is coming down right on top of Chambliss. I don't think I've ever seen anything funnier than his feet popping up and down, that partition caving in on top of him, and him still yelling, "What's going on out there?"

Somewhere along the way, though, Goose took a swing, hit the partition, and tore the ligaments on his pitching thumb. He went on the disabled list, and the fight became coast-to-coast news.

But it all worked out. Goose finished strong, the Yankees won the World Series over the Dodgers, and Goose is now a millionaire pitcher with the NL champion San Diego Padres. Johnson was last seen waiting for a fastball with the Texas Rangers, and Chambliss was with the Atlanta Braves—escapees, all, from the Bronx Zoo. And all with million-dollar contracts. So who says fighting doesn't pay off?

With my attitude, it's a wonder I didn't get into more fights when I was first coming up. Once I almost duked it out with Jim Fregosi, who later became one of my best friends.

We were with the Angels in the late '60s, and I was in center field. Fregosi was playing shortstop. Something happened, and we started yelling at each other. He had told me in no uncertain terms to do something, and I yelled back, "Shut up or I'll learn how to play shortstop too, and you'll be out of a job."

Now he was infuriated. He dropped his glove and started toward center after me. The umpire got there first, however, and there was no fight. And after the game—just like in the movies—Jimmy put his arm around me and said "You know, you're not such a bad kid after all . . . you've got a lot of spunk," and we became friends. We still keep in touch, and with the success he's had managing the Louisville Redbirds, I think it's only a matter of time before he's managing again in the big leagues.

This postscript: Fregosi took time to work with me and encourage me as a kid trying to make it. Piersall did the same. I just don't see that many players doing it today with youngsters. That's one thing great about Bill Russell of the Dodgers. Even though he was in danger of losing his shortstop job, he was always there helping and encouraging Dave Anderson and Mariano Duncan. That takes class.

Russell, in fact, took a lot of heat during his years in Los

Angeles. I've heard him called everything from "the worst shortstop in baseball" to "overrated," but it wasn't true. He was a very good shortstop and a helluva clutch player for a lot of years with the Dodgers. And the irony of it all is that he took more criticism than any member of that infield, which remained together longer (more than eight years) than any in the history of baseball—Steve Garvey at first, Davey Lopes at second, Russell at short, Ron Cey at third—and yet, by the end of the 1982 season, he was the only one still with the Dodgers.

Not that I didn't have some fun with Russell. There were times when I was all over him. After he'd make an error, I'd take his glove and put a Band-Aid on it or maybe Mercurochrome. Then I'd tape some aspirins into the pocket.

Once, after Bill made four errors in an exhibition game at Vero Beach, I went out early the next day, roped off the seats behind first base, and placed sandbags in front of the fence. Then I put up a sign that read: "Enter at your risk. Bill Russell is playing shortstop today. All seats 25 cents."

I would steal Russell's clean sanitary socks almost every day. And on the days I didn't do it, somebody else would, just so they could watch Russell blame me.

One of the best ways to trash a man's fielding glove is by putting peanut shells down into the fingers. His first reaction is almost always the same: He drops it because something foreign is in there.

Did I say glove? I played so little in 1985 spring training with the Dodgers that finally I went to Lasorda and asked about it.

"I want you to be waiting for that special moment, our field-goal kicker," said Lasorda. "I want you to stand around all game, then come in to save the game in the last second."

That sounded sort of romantic. But I then asked:

"Does that mean I don't have to bring a glove on the field?"

And he answered: "You ever see a field-goal kicker with a glove?"

" Baseball trivia question for the ages: What do Tom Lasorda, Danny Ozark, Jim Frey, Lee Elia, Chuck Tanner, Dick Williams, Billy Martin, Roger Craig, Bob Lemon, Lefty Phillips, Bill Rigney, Jim Bunning, Rocky Bridges, Marty Marion, Joe Adcock, Bobby Wine, and Sherm Lollar have in common?

Answer: They all survived managing me. "

6
MANAGERS
I HAVE
TERRORIZED

*"You mean to say that I'm the only manager who never
thought Johnstone was funny? Well, you're right."*
Jim Frey

Blame it on Ramon Lora. Why else would anyone want
to lock Tommy Lasorda in his bedroom and make him
miss breakfast?

Or maybe it was the heat, or the fact that we were
champions of all baseball. Were the Los Angeles Dodgers
complacent following our 1981 World Series victory over
the New York Yankees?

Whatever the reasons, spring training for the Dodgers
by mid-March 1982, in my opinion, had been too quiet.
Much too quiet. We had been rowdy enough the year
before, with the mysterious Green Hornet—purveyor of
practical jokes—a frequent Dodgertown visitor. But for
some reason, there hadn't been many laughs in the clubhouse this spring, and I was getting the blame.

Why me? That's where Lora comes into the picture. He
was trying to make the club as a right-handed pinch hitter
and third catcher. And there were some, particularly
among the press corps, who felt I might lose my spot on the

25-man roster to Lora. That's why I was being so quiet, they said. I was afraid to offend anyone.

Right.

The first thing I did was steal a master room key from the Dodgertown office. It was a caper in itself, including the bribe of an employee to return it. But I had to have entry to the room of Lasorda, our esteemed manager. Finding the room empty was no problem. There was no food there and nobody to listen to him talk, so why would Lasorda want to be there?

While Tommy was out to dinner, I slipped into Room 112 and removed the mouthpiece speakers from both telephones. Phase one was complete. Lasorda returned about midnight, tried to make some calls, couldn't figure out why he could hear the operator but she couldn't hear him. He spent the next two hours in Dodger publicist Steve Brener's room, using his phone—probably calling Don Rickles and all of his maitre d' pals around the country.

Meanwhile, the Green Hornet waited.

Finally, at about 2 A.M., Lasorda returned to his room for some sleep. At 4 A.M. we struck.

With help from catcher Steve Yeager, I tied a four-way sailor's knot around a palm tree, 30 feet from Lasorda's front door. The other end was noosed onto the door, which opened inward. The line was so taut you could have hung clothes on it.

Now came the fun. When Lasorda tried opening his only door in the morning, the line only got tighter. Then he picked up the phones and started yelling at the girl on the switchboard. She couldn't hear him, of course—and Lasorda finally began realizing the significance of his entrapment.

He might have to miss breakfast.

The team bus for an exhibition game in Orlando, you see, was to depart at 8 A.M., and certainly the manager was expected to be on it, with or without breakfast.

Now Tommy started screaming out the window (no way he could escape through the slats with that body). But Room 112 is located at the very end of Dodgertown, in a corner next to the laundry. Nobody walked past. One of our pitchers, Ted Power, lived in Room 108 about four doors down and later reported that he was awakened by the cries for help.

About that time, pitcher Steve Howe approached Lasorda's room to ask for permission to drive to Orlando separately with his wife. Hearing Lasorda, however, he simply turned around and told his wife to go home.

Finally, scout Ralph Avila heard Lasorda, looked through the window, and saw him with a chair in his hand, ready to smash the glass.

"Don't do it," shouted Avila, untying the rope.

But the rescue came too late. Tommy had been locked in his room for more than 30 minutes, and it was too late for breakfast. He was livid.

One thing about Lasorda. He can put on a great act, but I can always tell when he is truly angry. He won't look at you. He can't. And when I got onto the bus that morning, he screamed, "Go to the back of the bus," but he wouldn't look at me.

"Whatever happened to 'Hi, how are you, and good morning'?" I asked. I soon found out about what kind of good day it was going to be. Tommy didn't wait long to prove that payback can be a bitch.

Following the three-hour bus ride to Orlando, he put me at first base. In the first inning, I scrambled for a ball hit over first base, tagged the bag for a great play, and felt like a million bucks. After that, working with two-and-a-half hours of sleep, it was all downhill.

First there was a wide throw from shortstop. I caught the ball but forgot to touch the base. Then I missed the ball on a pickoff throw from the pitcher. Then there was a foul pop-up between Yeager and myself.

I caught the ball near the first base railing, then flipped it to Yang. At least, I thought I was flipping it to Yang. But he had turned away, and the ball went into an old lady's lap in the front row. The umpire ruled that I threw the ball into the stands and allowed the runner to go from first to second.

Lasorda, meanwhile, was not about to let me come out of the game. In fact, he was inside the clubhouse stealing my street clothes. I had to ride back from Orlando in my undershorts—once again persecuted without proof of guilt.

Baseball trivia question for the ages: What do Tom Lasorda, Danny Ozark, Jim Frey, Lee Elia, Chuck Tanner, Dick Williams, Billy Martin, Roger Craig, Bob Lemon, Lefty Phillips, Bill Rigney, Jim Bunning, Rocky Bridges, Marty Marion, Joe Adcock, Bobby Wine, and Sherm Lollar have in common?

Answer: They all survived managing me.

I believe I'm qualified to talk about managers. I think I know the difference between a good one and a bad one.

A manager can't hit, run, or throw for you. That's the first thing to remember. But he can motivate you, and there is nothing more important.

People talk about the managerial greatness of the late Casey Stengel of the Yankees. But let's be honest. You could have sent those Yankee teams onto the field and won. They didn't bunt, hit-and-run, steal, or anything. When you've got guys hitting 25–50 home runs a year, you don't need that other stuff.

I keep hearing, too, about the genius of Earl Weaver, who retired at Baltimore. In a way, I'm sorry I never got to play for him because I heard a lot of feisty things about him. But he always had great clubs, especially great pitching.

I prefer to judge managers who don't have the best

players. They have to motivate. A player doesn't necessarily have to like the manager, but he must respect him to be motivated.

How does a manager win that respect? First, he should be honest with the players—tell them their roles and have an open-door policy for talking out problems. Also, I prefer managers who can mingle with the players yet retain their respect. This isn't easy. There are players who pout if they're not in the lineup. There are players who try to use a manager's friendship to further their own careers.

Consider Chuck Tanner, who managed me 20 years ago in the minor leagues. He started the 1985 season managing Pittsburgh, having won 1,067 big league games and ranking 31st on the all-time managerial list.

When I was young and thought I knew everything, I never thought Tanner was a great manager. But, God, did he know how to motivate. He can make players perform beyond their capabilities.

A ball player, you see, should never try to do things he can't do. If you can't run very fast, why try to steal bases? If you strike out a lot, you shouldn't be trying to hit home runs. A good manager must learn those capabilities of his players and get the most out of what he has.

The great manager is the one who gets even more than is there.

Two other managers I wish I'd played for: Ralph Houk and John McNamara, the man who succeeded Houk with the Boston Red Sox. I've met few players who didn't respect McNamara.

I've also met few managers I couldn't terrorize.

Let's start with Lasorda of the Dodgers. He's 57, stands 5'9", weighs anywhere from 195 to 215 pounds, and can eat an entire lasagna while giving a television interview. He has been one of baseball's best ambassadors of goodwill and public relations for the last nine years.

But he really got mad when somebody pulled the tomato

switch on him. Some Italian donor had delivered these beautiful, huge, beefsteak tomatoes to Lasorda who placed them on top of his desk for everyone to admire. But during the game, the big tomatoes shrunk. That's the only explanation I could come up with, because when Lasorda came into his office after the game, there was a box of tiny cherry tomatoes sitting there.

That took care of any postgame interviews. You'd have thought somebody had stolen the key to Captain Queeg's strawberry locker.

Lasorda, though, can roll with the punches. (With his stomach, he could dress in stripes and roll on the White House lawn on Easter morning.) And I've learned to pick my spots with him. He would come strolling through the clubhouse on a Sunday morning in the greatest of moods, but by the time he got to his office, Reuss and I could have him screaming.

"I'm gonna quit coming in here on Sundays," he'd yell. "I'm gonna start going around the other way. I go to church, I come here happy, and you guys get me all tense and tight. I'm in knots, my stomach's driving me crazy, and you guys are driving me nuts."

Then he'd go into his office, eat something, and feel better.

It was Rick Monday's idea to put the makeup mirror in Lasorda's office. We found it in equipment manager Nobe Kawano's room. I have no idea how it got there. Maybe Don Rickles left it. Anyhow, we took Tommy's own desk out of his office and replaced it with this little desk with the makeup mirror, which had those little white bulbs all around the edges. That cost us two days of eating in his office. He said we shouldn't be fooling around with his personal belongings.

But that didn't stop us from clearing all the pictures out of his office—there must have been 200, mostly of Frank Sinatra—and all that we left on the bare walls were pictures of Don Stanhouse, Jerry Reuss, and me. It's not like we were trying to be anonymous.

Lasorda, of course, went into a tirade when he came in from batting practice. He layed it on big because he had an office full of Bo-bo's. (Baseball translation: *Bo-bo* is a hanger-on who follows a certain player or manager around and agrees with everything he says; often carries things or delivers things for player or manager.)

Just as Lasorda was reaching the climax of his speech, however, I interrupted and said:

"Hold it, Tommy. Calm down. Let me ask you one question, OK?"

"What, what, what?"

"How many games did those guys Sinatra and Rickles ever win for you?"

Harassing Lasorda is good therapy. You just have to know how to do it. Like the time in Montreal when Don Sutton was still pitching with the Dodgers. He walks into Tommy's office and says, "I just want you to know, Skip, that whatever happens, I had nothing to do with it."

"What are you talking about?"

"I just want you to know I didn't have anything to do with it."

"To do with what? What are you talking about?" screamed Lasorda, but Sutton has already gone.

Then the second guy comes along. It's Jerry Reuss: "I didn't do it, Tommy. I didn't do it."

"What in the hell are you talking about?" yells Lasorda, but Reuss is heading out the door.

Now we go onto the field for batting practice, and I come up to Lasorda and say, "Tommy, hey ... we've been friends for a long time, and I appreciate all you've done for me, but I really had nothing to do with what happened."

"OK, fuckers," he yells, "What's going on?"

So now we've got a flight—the end of the road trip—and all night long he keeps asking us, "What are you guys talking about?" He asks the PR man, Steve Brener. He asks the traveling secretary, Billy De Lury. Nobody could help him. Why? Because there was nothing. We just wanted to harass him.

Like the time in Atlanta when Derrel Thomas was playing center field and Lasorda was trying to motion for him to play deeper. Instead, Derrel wouldn't move. Even Reggie Smith was screaming at him from the dugout. Finally, when Derrel sat down against the center-field fence during a pitching change, Reggie blew up.

He came into the locker room after the game, slammed his hand into the Coke machine, and cut his hand so badly he needed stitches. So then there were words among Reggie, Derrel, and Lasorda, but it was supposed to be kept a secret, right? Instead, the whole blowup ended up in the paper with an "unnamed player" quoted as giving the information.

So Lasorda then held a meeting the next day and started screaming, "Who the fuck is this unnamed player who's telling things to the press? Stand up and be counted. Who is it?"

It sounded to me like a case for the pressure-busters. So Steve Garvey, of all people, Reuss, Don Stanhouse, and I went back to the hotel that night and wrote this formal letter to Lasorda:

"Dear Uncle Tom," it began. "We love you, and we love the Dodgers, and we would do nothing to disrupt the team. We love you, Tom. We didn't mean it.—The Unnamed Player."

The thing to remember about Lasorda and managers like him is that they encourage laughter in the clubhouse. In the immortal words of Danny Ozark: "You can't play baseball with a tight asshole."

Ozie was a successful manager at Philadelphia—594 wins, 510 losses (.538) over a seven-year period (1973–79), yet, like most managers, he was fired. Maybe it was because he won three division championships ('76, '77, '78) but failed to get into the World Series. I think they just wanted to make a change, and Ozark caught the blame.

Or maybe it was the heat he kept catching over his Ozarkisms.

Danny could fracture the English language, and Bill Conlin, baseball writer for the *Philadelphia Daily News*— and, in my opinion, the best in the country—became a chronicler and collector of Ozarkisms. Some of his and my favorites from Danny Ozark:

- When asked if there might be a morale problem on the Phillies: "This team's morality is not a factor."
- When his job was in jeopardy and general manager Paul Owens was making trips with the team, he said Owens's presence "was not intimidating and, furthermore, I will not be cohorsed."
- His evaluation of infielder Mike Andrews: "His limitations are limitless."
- After being swept three games by Atlanta in 1976, he said: "It is beyond my apprehension."
- After the Phils led by 15½ games, lost 10 in a row, and saw the lead shrink to almost nothing, he said: "Even Napoleon had his Watergate."
- After managing well and outfinessing an opponent, Danny accepted press plaudits by saying: "Who knows what evil lurks in the hearts of men except the Shadow?"
- When asked why he never gave straight answers: "Don't you know I'm a fascist? You know, a guy who says one thing and means another?"
- Asked if he had problems with his players: "Contrary to popular belief, I have always had a wonderful repertoire with my players."

- Once we had six games to play but trailed by seven, and he figured that if we won all of our remaining games, we could still tie.

And when asked why the Phils had a better win-loss record at home than on the road, Danny said: "It's simple. We play more games at home than we do on the road."

Huh? You can see why he caught so much heat from the press.

Once we had a meeting before playing Cincinnati—1975, the Big Red Machine—and we've got Lefty (Steve Carlton) pitching. But Lefty wouldn't come to the meeting to go over Cincinnati hitters. After the meeting, I could understand why. The meeting went like this:

"Pete Rose: great fastball hitter, first fastball hitter, line drive hitter, keep him high and tight, low and away, don't give him anything good to hit.

"Ken Griffey: good fastball hitter, likes that first fastball, curves in the dirt or high and tight, keep the fastball away from him, he can spray it.

"Joe Morgan: great fastball hitter, first ball hitter, good power, can hit it out. Throw the ball high and tight, low and away, don't give him anything to hit. Make him swing at bad pitches.

"Johnny Bench: good fastball hitter, first fastball hitter, can drive it out of the park, don't give him anything to hit. Curve balls, down and away."

That's when Larry Bowa interrupted and said, "Say Danny, so far we've got the bases loaded and one run in. What do we do now?"

That was the year, 1976, when we clinched the division in Montreal, then flew into St. Louis for a series that really didn't matter. So Ozark calls this meeting and says "Now that we've clinched the division, I want you guys to relax out there, keep in shape, and don't get hurt. But some of you have personal milestones to reach, so let's go after

them. I'm behind you. Mike [Schmidt], I want you to get 40
home runs. Lefty, I want you to win 20 games."

So in the second game of the series, I hit a ball into the
gap that could have been a triple. Nothing automatic, but
maybe. But I'm just two doubles behind Pete Rose for the
league lead (40–38), and I stop at second base.

Ozark chewed my ass for days. Such is the fate of a
scapegoat. There were other times when he gambled on
my bat against left-handers and came out looking like a
genius.

The point is, these guys know how to laugh, and I make
it my personal responsibility to see that they do. But I had
a hard time getting Cubs' manager Jim Frey to relax.
Frankly, I don't think he thought I was very funny. Not that
he's not a good guy. Everybody, in fact, tells me that he's a
helluva guy—especially away from the clubhouse. But
that's a pretty serious clubhouse in Chicago.

At first, I thought it would be different under Frey. Like
the time in spring training, 1984, when the boss, Dallas
Green, went on a rampage and decided to chew out the
entire clubhouse.

Dallas, of course, can be pretty imposing. He's at least
6'6"—John Wayne of the National League—and when he
was storming around the clubhouse in Mesa, Arizona (I
think we were 3 and 13 at the time), he did get our
attention. Frey, meanwhile, is leaning on one of the saw-
horses at the other end of the room, just listening.

Finally, Green stops screaming and storms out of the
room, slamming the door. Then Frey comes down into the
clubhouse, looks around, and sees that most of the guys
don't know what to say. We were in shock.

"Well, that's kind of a bummer way to start off the day,"
he said and everybody broke up. And I said to myself, "It's
going to be fun to be around this guy."

But it didn't work out that way. Maybe it had something
to do with the pressure from above. Maybe it was because

Frey didn't think I produced (.288 but no home runs and only three RBIs). Or maybe it was the pressure of trying to bring a winner to a franchise that hadn't won in 37 years. Whatever the reasons, Frey gave out no-nonsense signals.

But isn't there a difference between no nonsense and not having any fun? Like the time I went into my "Old Man in Baseball" routine. It was during a rain delay, and my old team (now my new team again), the Dodgers, were in Wrigley Field. I put on a Lasorda uniform shirt, stuffed it with pillows, turned my cap, and waddled across the field toward the Dodger dugout. The fans loved it, and Dodger pitching coach Ron Perranoski almost choked he laughed so hard. Then I waddled back across the field and sat on the Cubs' bench.

Then Frey came out, saw me, and said, "You're not going out there like that, are you?"

I said, "No, Jim, I wouldn't think of it."

On another occasion, one of those benefit charity events where the Cubs really raise a lot of money, everybody on the team was to pose for a group picture in tuxedos.

"Fuck the tuxedo," I said to myself and showed up dressed as entertainer Michael Jackson. Complete with the sunglasses, the glove, and the silver socks. So what was Frey going to do, make me pose for the picture in my underwear? Everybody else loved it, and he just shook his head. The best part, though, is that we ended up sitting just one table apart at dinner, and people kept coming up to me by the dozens saying my outfit was great.

Understand one thing, though. I didn't leave the Cubs with any bitterness, even though I was cut on August 31 to make room for Davey Lopes, who they felt would give them more versatility for the playoffs. It was a personnel move that cost me another postseason appearance, but Dallas kept me in uniform (I was "shower coach," in charge of pointing players toward the showers) through September and October. It was appreciated.

As for Frey and his managing, well, let's just put it this way. I wouldn't have walked Tony Gwynn to pitch to Steve Garvey in the fourth game of the 1984 National League playoffs. Certainly not twice, I don't care if Gwynn hit .690 during the season. You've got to show me he can do it in the clutch, when the pressure's on. It's a proven fact, time after time after time, that Garvey has hit in the clutch during the playoffs. I don't care if Gwynn's hitting 1.000. You still have to pitch to him.

I wouldn't have saved Rick Sutcliffe, either, for game five instead of pitching him in game four. Nor would I have left Rick in the fifth game as long as Frey did. But that's second guessing, and anybody can do that, especially in Chicago.

One *Chicago Tribune* sportswriter, Bernie Lincicome, even wrote that the Cubs lost to the San Diego Padres because they "choked."

Choked? I look at what happened to the Cubs in San Diego this way:

- In game three in San Diego, we were overwhelmed by San Diego fans. I really believe it.
- In game four we were beaten, almost single-handedly, by Steve Garvey.
- In game five we led, 3–0 with the Cy Young Award winner on the mound. You can make any further judgments on your own.

In Chicago, in retrospect, though, certainly I have no sour grapes to peddle. Playing in Wrigley Field was one of the biggest thrills of my life, and I found the Chicago people, when I played with the Sox and Cubs, to be some of the nicest you could possibly want to meet.

Getting released from the Cubs before the playoffs of 1984 did hurt, but it's part of baseball. They were hardly getting a virgin.

Maybe some day Jim Frey and I can meet away from the ball park and have a few laughs. But I don't think I'll wear a white glove or stuff any pillows under my shirt. For Jimmy, I think I may need a different routine.

Maybe some day, too, Lee Elia will manage again in the major leagues. He was a scapegoat in Chicago.

Elia was a blue-collar manager, a man who would fight like crazy for his ball players because he had been one himself. He just didn't have the tact to handle the press.

He took a makeshift roster of players in 1982 and part of 1983, before he got fired and, in my opinon, he did a helluva job. I know his record: 73–89 in 1982 and 54–69 before being replaced by interim Charlie Fox in 1983, but he still did a helluva job. He had a real working knowledge of the game and was a super person to be around. All he needed was experience.

Elia went along with my antics (including having so much fun with Penguin) because he felt it would make things better for the club. With all the strange faces we had in the clubhouse, it was crucial that we try to bring these guys together as a team. I've always been an Elia guy, always will be. He just needed polish. I looked at the guys we had and those who didn't play up to form, and I felt sorry for him because I knew we had all let him down.

A lot of people believe that his infamous clubhouse blowup in front of writers and radio microphones (44 bleeps in a 400-word tirade) eventually cost him his job. But did it? I don't think so. In fact, we caught fire after that and were only four games out of first place at All-Star break, and there were big signs behind the dugout that read, "Elia for Mayor." Everything had been forgotten, and it had only been six weeks since he ripped the Cubs' fans.

But after the All-Star game, we sank like a torpedoed rowboat, and Lee was history. Maybe if he hadn't had that earlier blowup he could have saved his job. I don't know.

But I do believe that, if we'd kept winning, Elia wouldn't have been fired.

What did the Cubs' manager say on April 13, 1983, following a 4–3 loss to the Dodgers, which caused such an uproar? Well, for the sake of accuracy, I'll give it to you straight. No bleeps, ma'am, just the monologue, direct from the unsoaped mouth of Lee Elia and straight from his heart:

"Fuck those fuckin' fans who come out here and say they're Cub fans that are supposed to be behind you, rippin' every fuckin' thing you do. I'll tell you one fuckin' thing, I hope we get fuckin' hotter than shit, just to stuff it up them 3,000 fuckin' people that show up every fuckin' day, because if they're the real Chicago fuckin' fans, they can kiss my fuckin' ass right downtown and PRINT IT.

"They're really, really behind you around here . . . my fuckin' ass. What the fuck am I supposed to do, go out there and let my fuckin' players get destroyed every day and be quiet about it? For the fuckin' nickel-dime people who turn up? The motherfuckers don't even work. That's why they're out at the fuckin' game. They oughta go out and get a fuckin' job and find out what it's like to go out and earn a fuckin' living. Eighty-five percent of the fuckin' world is working. The other fifteen percent come out here. A fuckin' playground for the cocksuckers. Rip them motherfuckers. Rip them fuckin' cocksuckers like the fuckin' players. We got guys bustin' their fuckin' ass, and them fuckin' people boo. And that's the Cubs? My fuckin' ass. They talk about the great fuckin' support the players get around here. I haven't seen it this fuckin' year. Everybody associated with this organization have been winners their whole fuckin' life. Everybody. And the credit is not given in that respect.

"Alright, they don't show because we're 5 and 14 . . . and unfortunately, that's the criteria of them dumb 15 motherfuckin' percent that come out to day baseball. The other 85 percent are earning a living. I tell you, it'll take more than a 5 and 12 or 5 and 14 to destroy the

makeup of this club. I guarantee you that. There's some
fuckin' pros out there that wanna win. But you're stuck
in a fuckin' stigma of the fuckin' Dodgers and the Phillies
and the Cardinals and all that cheap shit. It's unbelievable. It really is. It's a disheartening fuckin' situation that
we're in right now. Anybody who was associated with the
Cub organization four or five years ago that came back
and sees the multitude of progress that's been made will
understand that if they're baseball people, that 5 and 14
doesn't negate all that work. We got 143 fuckin' games
left.

"What I'm tryin' to say is don't rip them fuckin' guys
out there. Rip me. If you wanna rip somebody, rip my
fuckin' ass. But don't rip them fuckin' guys cause they're
givin' everything they can give. And right now they're
tryin' to do more than God gave 'em, and that's why we
make the simple mistakes. That's exactly why."

Whew. Now you can see why the ball players felt Lee
Elia was behind them. But supporting our simple mistakes
with 36 *fuckin'*s, two *shit*s, four *motherfuckers*, and two
cocksuckers, without taking a deep breath, translated into
a big mistake for Lee.

Yet, what if the Cubs had won the division title in 1983
instead of one year later? I'm guessing Elia still would have
been manager. Maybe even the mayor of Chicago.

Then there was Billy Martin. He was manager of the New
York Yankees when I joined them in 1978. He also got fired
in 1978. I can understand why. In those days, Billy was self-
destructing.

The first weekend I joined the Yanks, coming over from
the Phillies in that strange trade for pitcher Rawly Eastwick, we're having problems against the California Angels.
Martin comes into the clubhouse after the loss on Sunday,
June 14, and he looks like a ghost. I'm thinking, "It's just a
game," but even I knew this was no time to say anything.

The next thing I see is a chair flying out of his office. It hits the wall. Then out comes a lamp. Then the table that the lamp was on. It hits the wall, too.

"What the hell is goin' on?" I ask Gene Michaels, a coach.

"Billy is depressed," says Gene.

And when Billy got depressed—whether over his health or over losing or over the atmosphere created by owner George Steinbrenner—he got into the booze. And certainly he had plenty of chances to get depressed. When he was sober, he was one of the greatest guys you'd ever want to know.

But consider the night Billy got fired because he took a shot at both Reggie Jackson and Steinbrenner by saying, "One's a born liar, and the other's convicted."

The Yanks were in Chicago, and after the game Billy had gone upstairs to drink in the Bard's Room, a hospitality room for the press, visiting scouts, and friends of White Sox management. It began innocently enough, with Billy having a few pops with announcer Harry Caray and some writers—but by the time he left for O'Hare Airport, he was on his way to trouble. Unfortunately, the plane was delayed and Billy had time for a visit to the terminal cocktail lounge before departure.

Two New York reporters heard his comment about Jackson and Steinbrenner, and although they surely knew he was soused, wrote it nevertheless. Another Billy Martin chapter had been written, with more to come.

Wherever there was controversy, there was Reggie Jackson. A lot of the guys simply didn't like him, and I'm sure they had their reasons. But in certain situations, there is no one I'd rather have going to the plate for my team than Reggie. What's he got, 503 home runs? That's a lot of home runs.

I had just joined the Yankees in 1978 when Mary Jayne made a trip to Baltimore with us and met Reggie for the first time. She loved it. But he also said something then that seemed funny, yet, seems a little sad now with the telling.

We had been walking around the little shops in our hotel—just the three of us—while waiting for the team bus. We bought some ice cream and just sat and talked. Then I had to return to the room for something I'd forgotten, and Reggie and Mary Jayne stayed to talk longer. I guess they had quite a conversation.

Anyhow, later that night during the chartered flight to Oakland, Reggie came up to talk with us.

"What are you guys going to do in Oakland?" he asked.

"We don't know."

"Well, look, if you need a car, just let me know, I've got friends out here with agencies. I could help you out."

Then he said, "I can do wonders for my friends, I just don't have very many."

At the time, I thought it was funny even though he was very sincere.

My fondest memory of wearing a Yankee uniform: outfielder Mickey Rivers, in one automobile, being chased around the parking lot of Yankee Stadium by his irate wife, who was in another; I think they partially or totally damaged 11 other cars in the lot during the chase. Where else but Yankee Stadium can you play Bronx Bumper Pool?

Frankly, I felt I was one of the sanest people in the Yankee clubhouse. Bronx Zoo was a good name. There were jealousies, fear of and loathing for the owner, immense media presure, and the unpredictably volatile condition of the manager.

On top of that, I didn't play much (65 at bats in 1978, 48 in 1979) and didn't hit (.262 and .208) when I did play. Even the arrival of Bob Lemon as manager didn't improve my situation. Impending free agency was the only answer. I used it to escape from the zoo.

Lemon, incidentally, is another of baseball's good people. I've known him since I was a kid and he was an instructor for the Angels in a weekend league in southern

California. Then I got him again as manager in Triple A in Seattle, and one day he called me into his office to tell me I'd been called up to the major leagues.

I could hardly wait. This was my chance, and this Hall-of-Famer was going to give me advice on how to succeed in the big leagues. Well, he did. He talked to me for 45 minutes about how to handle the females who would be chasing me. I couldn't believe my ears. I kept waiting for him to tell me what pitches I might see. Instead, he talked about all the girls who try to catch ball players. I'll never forget that conversation. It was wonderful. He didn't say one word about baseball.

When I played briefly under Dick Williams with the Oakland A's in 1973, he was all business. After all, he had one of the better teams in the history of baseball. If you were doing well, he liked you. If you weren't in the starting lineup, he preferred that you keep your mouth shut. For me, that wasn't too easy.

Remember, though, that I was a Charlie Finley salvage job. Williams sort of ignored me and let the coaches handle any problems I might have with Williams. I felt like I was in the Army. But I wasn't about to go AWOL, even though I wasn't one of his fans.

He has changed as a manager. He's become more tolerant. It wouldn't be fair for me to judge, but I get the feeling that he just tolerates having Steve Garvey with the Padres. I don't think Williams particularly likes Garvey's image, but there isn't a helluva lot he can do about it. The owners like Garv. Besides, he's my pal.

Roger Craig was managing the Padres back in 1979 when I came over from the Yankees. You couldn't have asked for a smoother relationship. I walked into the clubhouse, and he said, "Great to have you. Where do you want to play?"

After my experience with the Yankees, I wasn't sure I

had heard him right. I mumbled something about not caring, that I just wanted to play.

"Can you play outfield?" he said.

"Sure, I'm an outfielder."

"Where do you want to play?"

"Well, I can play right or left."

"Can you play in center?"

"Sure, why not?"

I played center field that night. It was like I could have pitched if I had told him I wanted to pitch. Roger was that desperate for players. The Padres finished 58–93 that year and Roger was fired. I filed for free agency and landed with the Dodgers. But they didn't ask me where I wanted to play.

Perhaps the most knowledgeable baseball man I ever played under was Lefty Phillips, who succeeded Bill Rigney as manager of the Angels in 1969 and kept the job through 1971.

Lefty had only one problem. He could not communicate. He just couldn't sit down and talk with you. He either had a speech impediment or asthma or both, and on top of that he chewed tobacco. He really chewed tobacco. Nobody could ever understand what he was saying. Lefty is the only guy I ever knew who could give a 10-minute speech and leave everybody with a question mark on his face.

He kept that tobacco in his mouth so long every day (and maybe all night) that a ring would form around his mouth. And he would have spit marks all over his uniform. After a person-to-person conversation with Lefty, you had to go to the laundry. He was a super-nice guy, but it's difficult to gain the respect of a player when you're spraying him with Red Man.

Lefty wore these shoes two sizes too big—so big his toes would curl up—and when he walked to the mound he looked like he was wearing Aladdin lamps. Also, he had no ass. None. So his pants would hang down like he had taken a dump in them. So there he would go to the mound, wearing those little pixie shoes and his pants drooping with nothing to hold them up. I mean those shoes were so big that when the front spike hit the ground, it would flop. Lefty knew baseball, but he sure looked and sounded funny.

One of my favorites, of course, was Bill Rigney—probably because he was my first big league manager. I really thought he was cool. He'd always wear sunglasses for TV games, golf slacks, and golf sweaters—real *GQ* stuff—but he liked to have fun.

The only time he'd really argue with umpires was if it was a TV game. Then he'd go out and put on a marvelous show, stomping and kicking dirt and the whole thing.

And when he wanted to talk to me or any other rookie, he'd always yell, "Hey, you," or "Hey, number 10," or "Hey, kid, I read about you. Show me what you can do." In my third season with the Angels, he called me Jay, and I had to turn around to see whom he wanted. Who, me?

It was Rigney who assigned me as a rookie to room with Jim Piersall.

"I like my kids rooming with veterans so they can learn something," said Rigney. So I roomed with Piersall and, yes, I learned things. All kinds of things.

I even learned about baseball. Jimmy would wake up in the middle of the night and say, "Hey, are you asleep?"

"No, I always lie awake at 3:00 A.M. What do you want?"

"Did you see that play that so-and-so made out there today? Did you see what he did wrong?"

"Are you nuts?"

That wasn't exactly the right thing to say to Jim Piersall, of course. So I'd have to recreate in my mind the play he was talking about. Then I'd have to give an opinion about what he should have done. And if Jim was satisfied with my answer, he'd allow me to go back to sleep.

Rigney was a great motivator, but Chuck Tanner was the master. Tanner could motivate water out of a rock. He could also squeeze gravel out of it. He's the strongest man I've ever met in baseball.

I was playing for him in the minor leagues one year, and he was coaching third base. I'll never forget it because he damned-near choked me to death.

I had just cleared the bases with a rocket off the right-center-field wall. I'm really pumping toward third base for a triple, and I hear Chuck yelling, "Get down, get down," as I start my slide, and I beat the tag by just a hair.

Tanner is so ecstatic that he pulls me up by one hand and starts dusting me off with the other. He's holding me up in the air, and I'm yelling "Chuck, put me down, put me down." But he keeps yelling, "Way to go, Jay, way to go," and he's choking the shit out of me while dusting me off with the other hand. That's how strong he was. He didn't even know his own strength.

I've seen Tanner lift other guys off the ground and hang them on hooks just like an old coat. His favorite trick was to shake hands with somebody—maybe a sportswriter— and see if he could grip hard enough to send the guy to his knees. If you had a ring on, he'd crush your fingers.

With the White Sox, my roomie was catcher Tom Egan, and he was a funny guy. Tanner, though, was trying to whip us into shape, and there were some things he wouldn't accept. Like the time Egan struck out on three straight pitches and looked bad doing it.

Still at home plate, Tom clicked his heels to attention, raised his bat, and placed it alongside his body into an imaginary scabbard, just like a soldier, and marched back toward the dugout.

We thought it was funny, but Tanner didn't. He chased Egan all the way into the clubhouse and into the shower. They were running around in circles in the shower with Egan yelling, "Chuck, Chuck, I was only kidding," and Tanner yelling, "If you ever do anything like that again, I'll kill you."

Tanner did a remarkable job of managing Richie (or Dick—take your pick) Allen with the White Sox in 1972, even though he caught a lot of criticism for giving him preferential treatment. And there's no question that he did. But what a season Allen had: 37 home runs and 113 RBIs in 148 games. He also walked 99 times and hit .308.

Allen was amazing. I've seen him play the first game of a doubleheader, then get into a whirlpool with a bottle of scotch, only to be called out during the second game to hit a home run.

To be honest, Tanner allowed Allen to do almost anything he wanted. He seldom took batting practice. Allen would prefer to stay in the clubhouse and practice his batting stance in front of a mirror. Then, about 20 minutes before game time, he'd come onto the field and take some warm-up throws. His logic was simple: If he had hit successfully the night before, and he had remembered the "feeling" he didn't want to change it with meaningless batting practice.

But he always showed up to play, and in my 16-plus years in major league baseball, I'd be hard-pressed to come up with one man who had a greater single season than Allen had with the White Sox in 1972. So even though Tanner got that production out of him for just one year, he must have been doing something right.

I never played under Walter Alston, but they tell me he was also a manager of great physical strength and volatile temper.

I do remember Walter telling me that he once called a

sportswriter, Maury Allen of New York, into the clubhouse to discuss an article Allen had written. And Walter, knowing his own temper, immediately took off his spikes. Why? So that if they got into a fight, Alston wouldn't be sliding out of control on the concrete floor.

Bill Buckner once lost his temper and threw his helmet against the wall of the dugout. It bounced off and grazed Alston on the head. "If you ever hit me with that helmet again," said Alston, "I'll fine you $500."

Now, a couple of weeks later, Buckner throws his helmet again and it's bouncing down the dugout floor toward Alston. Buckner ran, stumbled, crawled, and slid on his belly to grab the helmet just inches before it would have touched Alston.

Maury Wills, now a base-running and bunting instructor with the Dodgers, tells his favorite story about Alston:

"We had just lost a tough doubleheader in Pittsburgh— Sandy Koufax and Don Drysdale had both been beaten— and we're on the bus heading up the hill toward the Pittsburgh airport. But it was a dreadful bus—old, smelly, oily, no air conditioning, and really slow. Guys in the back of the bus were really complaining to Lee Scott, our traveling secretary. And just then the Pirates, heading out of town for a road trip, passed us in a new, air-conditioned bus. And somebody from the back of our bus yelled, 'Hey, we're going so slow there's a dog pissing on our tires.'

"Well, Walter had heard enough. He makes the bus driver stop the bus. Then he stands up, looks down the aisle, and says, 'I'm in charge of this bus. And I'm going to get off right now. If any of you fellows want to come outside and discuss this, please come out. You can come out one at a time or all together. Makes no difference to me. I'll be waiting.'

"With that, he walks off the bus. You could have heard a pin drop. Nobody moved. Then, after a few minutes, he got back on, sat down, and never said a word. For the rest of the ride to the airport, you never heard a quieter bus."

The only time I almost had to fight a manager was in the minor leagues. It was the same manager, Jim Bunning, who suspended me for going to the john.

This was 1974 I belonged to the Phillies, but because of roster problems, they had to send me to their Triple A team in Toledo, Ohio, to open the season.

"Just take a hotel room," I was told by GM Paul Owens. "You'll be right up."

I kept that hotel room (thank God for maids) for two months before joining the Phillies for the final 64 games of the 1974 season. It was the last assignment I was to spend in the minor leagues. It was also one of the stormiest.

Let's face it. I was stuck. The manager of the Toledo Mud Hens, Jim Bunning, also felt stuck with me. I knew I was headed for the big club, and he knew it, but that didn't mean he had to like having me around.

Bunning, you see, was a perfectionist. Eventually, he hoped to land the managerial job with the Phillies. This was his shot to strut his stuff.

But I was thrust upon him and he wasn't very happy about it. He would have preferred a roster of kids who said "yessir" and "nossir" rather than a guy who had already spent seven years in the major leagues. Let's face it. I had a little reputation, right? A little crazy, right? I was also obviously ahead of the other players as far as experience and ability, and I think Bunning resented having to work with me.

So we almost had a fight. We laugh about it now, but it was that close.

He had been trying to use me as the scapegoat to get the other players' attention—everything from bed checks to paying attention in team meetings—and finally, one day, he stood in front of my locker and said: "Go ahead. Stand up and take a punch. Go ahead, take the first punch. I dare you."

My entire career flashed before my eyes. Punch the manager? I came within a microsecond of it but didn't.

Why me? Well, it probably had something to do with my *U.S.S. Titanic* T-shirt.

The incident: We had a lot of young guys on the team. I was hitting OK (.315, 8 HRs, 57 games), but some of the younger fellows weren't. I was particularly interested in Dane Iorg and Jerry Martin. Both showed talent and promise.

But after about six weeks into the season, both Iorg and Martin went into a tailspin. The worse they hit, the more they pressed and the worse they hit. That's how it works.

Finally, Field Marshall Bunning (later, an unsuccessful candidate for governor of Kentucky), calls a team meeting. Now, let me repeat. Jim Bunning was a perfectionist. He simply couldn't understand why others couldn't emulate him. It's one of the oldest stories of unsuccessful managers in baseball.

"You're sinking faster than the *Titanic*," he told Iorg, in front of an assembled Toledo squad. "And you're not far behind," he said, pointing to Martin.

To me, this was wrong. Iorg and Martin were young, impressionable players with considerable promise. I felt that if the manager had a bitch with them, it should be voiced behind closed doors.

And I couldn't leave it alone. Surprise, right?

The first thing I did was get an old wet suit from Rod Clark, our third baseman. It wasn't much—an old, rubber-topped wet suit—but it served the purpose. Then I put a ski mask over my head and taped "*U.S.S. Titanic*" on the front of the suit.

I got in the outfield during batting practice, with this *U.S.S. Titanic* wet suit and ski mask, carrying an oar and pretending to be paddling. Catching fly balls wasn't easy.

Then I went toward the infield and dived into the tarp, as if I was trying to save myself. A lot of players laughed, Iorg and Martin no longer felt sorry for themselves, and Bunning—well, what do you think? He was livid.

But do you know what? They started hitting the ball again. I'm not taking credit for it. I'm just saying that many times a manager gets carried away with his own image of himself and puts too much pressure on his players.

By now, of course, Bunning and I were on a collision course. Once when the TV cameras were there I gave them my commando routine—crawling along the clubhouse floor and lobbing a baseball into the manager's office as if it were a hand grenade. He didn't think that was funny, either.

Finally, the last straw. He suspended me for taking a shit. No shit.

We were playing a doubleheader. I'd eaten some Mexican food the night before, and Montezuma was taking revenge. I got through the first game OK, but now it's time for game two, and I'm heading for the john. Like, every two minutes, I'm heading for the john. And Bunning is keeping an eye on me.

It's the first inning, our turn at bat, and I yell, "Holler when there's two outs," and I head for the can. Now it's two out and the third hitter Jerry Martin is up and I'm supposed to hit next. But I'm not there, and Bunning sees it. And just as I come running out of the bathroom it's my turn to go to the plate.

Sorry, Jay. Too late. The manager has sent up a pinch hitter.

"What the hell's going on?" I yell.

"Last straw," he yells back. "You're suspended."

He suspended me for 30 days, but I never got to serve the suspension. The Phillies needed me, called me up to the big club, and I never spent another day in the minor leagues.

Later, of course, we became good pals, and I have to

admit that he taught me a lesson: Never drop your drawers during an at-bat unless you're headed for the major leagues.

People have asked me whether I would someday consider managing a major league baseball team.

My first reaction: No way. I've seen too many come and go.

On the other hand, maybe I'd be more prepared to handle unusual situations within a clubhouse. Certainly I've been involved in a few.

Also, I like working with young players, especially when it comes to hitting instruction. There's no denying the satisfaction of being able to pass along something you've learned to a youngster with talent and willingness to work.

But manage? Maybe someday I'll change my mind, but right now I'd prefer to make my transition from the playing field into a broadcasting booth.

Broadcasters never get fired because the team loses, and I've never heard of one being locked in his room.

Lasorda keeps telling me he can't wait for the day that I become a big league manager, so he can come out and taunt me.

Don't hold your breath, Tommy.

"

Once I was interviewed on the "NBC Game of the Week," and I said, "I drove through Cleveland one day, but it was closed." The next thing I knew, the mayor of Cleveland called NBC and demanded an apology.

CHAPTER
7
UMPIRES
AND OTHER
FANATICS

"He is the only player I've ever managed who needs a beeper."

Tom Lasorda

I was a teenaged Red-Ass. And make sure that's with a capital *R* and a capital *A*. It's not an unusual story in professional sports.

As a kid, I always did well athletically. Almost all pro athletes did. It's tough to make it big without a head start.

I hit above .500 as a Little Leaguer, about the same in Pony League and .547 in high school. (Why is it that everybody remembers exactly, to the decimal point, what they hit in high school?) I just wasn't accustomed to making an out.

Then, all of a sudden, I was playing with people at the same level of ability as me. It became a different story. Instead of meeting one or two ball players just as good as you, you're meeting a bunch of them, and they're matching their talents against yours.

Consequently, I wasn't mature enough to handle it. Remember, now, I had signed on high school graduation night. That made me hot stuff.

But when I found myself in the big leagues (1966) at age 19 and unable to hit .300, that hot stuff turned to hot temper. Whenever I made an out, I got furious—not at the pitcher or anybody else, but at myself. I'd throw helmets, bats, anything I could get my hands on. It was a legit, bona fide, 100-percent case of teenage red-ass, and, like all teens, I had to grow out of it the hard way.

Only once, though—in 22 years of playing professional baseball—did an "attitude" problem hinder my career.

It was 1965, with the El Paso Sun Kings, and Chuck Tanner was the manager. The situation:

Arturo Mirando was our shortstop, and he spoke very poor English. Now the home plate umpire calls a bad pitch a strike, and Arturo is yelping in Spanish. I figure that's not good enough, so I start giving it to the ump from the dugout, along with a bunch of other guys. Well, Bruce Froemming is umpiring at first base, and if you think he has a short fuse now, you should have seen that little Milwaukee fireplug then. He listens only so long to my crap and gives me the thumb. So long and goodbye.

The only problem is that the game goes into extra innings. Bottom of the 12th, Amarillo gets a runner on second base, and he scores on a grounder up the middle into center field. We lose.

Now here comes Tanner into the clubhouse, and he starts screaming at me.

"If you're in center field, you throw that guy out at home by 20 feet and we don't lose. This was your fault!"

"How can you blame me for losing a game if I'm not in a game?" I yelled back and the argument continued.

Bottom line: When Tanner filled out his managerial report, he wrote that I was a poor fielder. I'm a poor fielder, and I wasn't even in the game? No matter. I was sent back to San Jose for the balance of the 1965 season. During the off-season, I went into a six-month program with the U.S. Marines and upon release, found myself assigned once again to play for Tanner in El Paso.

Oh, I almost forgot. Froemming claims the reason he ejected me from that game was that I gave him the finger. I don't remember that. Maybe I was just telling him that the Sun Kings were number one. Whatever, it was an umpire's ejection that cost me half a season at a higher level. Moral of the story? Red is a nasty color when dealing with umpires.

Umpires, you see, have one flashing button. They don't like to be shown up. Push that button, and you're pushing the button on your own ejection seat.

I've noticed too, during my aging process, that the young umpires are far less tolerant than the older guys. Frankly, I think some of the newer umpires are trying to take shortcuts to make names for themelves. Some of these guys you can't even talk with. It's ridiculous.

Is there a difference in the umpiring of American League and National League games? For a hitter, you bet there is. The American League is a high-ball league. It always has been, and it's because American League umpires always had the chest protector on the outside. The guys from the NL put the chest protector inside their shirts, and they can get down lower on pitches.

Example: Dave Goltz came from the Minnesota Twins of the American League to the Dodgers of the National. He started throwing those chest-high pitches and never got them. Goltzy, of course, was supposed to be a sinker-ball pitcher, but he missed getting those high strike calls.

The only guy I ever knew who could get away with a high strike was Don Sutton. I've never been sure why.

As far as myself, I found problems with all the off-speed stuff they throw in the American League. That, and the fact that I spent the first seven years there and didn't really know how to hit. Finally, when I went into the National

League, I was hitting well, and I pride myself on drilling the good fastball.

So when I look at my American League batting average (.243) compared to that in the National (.289), I always have to remind myself that it was more than just fastballs (NL) against off-speed (AL). It was also learning to hit from Benny Lefebvre during the middle of my career.

Enough digression. We were talking about umpires, and let's get back to Frank (Helmet Head) Umont, umpire of my greatest triumph.

Actually, Frank is a sweetheart of a guy. He's kind of a gruff, Deputy Dog type of guy and I guess that's where he got his nickname, because he had this giant head.

I gave him a wonderful hotfoot.

This was back in the early '70s of course, before hotfoots became passé. We were in Chicago at Comiskey Park, and the umpires would have to come down into the dugout tunnel for a drink of water. Helmet Head was a perfect target.

While Umont was bending over to take a swig of water, I took a cigarette, placed a piece of chewing gum toward the lit part of the cigarette, and put it right where his corn would be on the outside part of the shoe.

Now he's back out at home plate, and remember what I said about the outside chest protectors? He's trying to get down for balls and strikes, and his foot is sticking out. Now he starts to wiggle it, and everybody in the dugout is watching. Now it's really starting to get hot, and he's jumping up and down at home plate, still trying to call balls and strikes.

The manager, of course, had no idea what was going on, and he couldn't understand why everybody in the dugout was laughing.

Actually, I've given a number of hotfoots in my day, and it's not that easy. You have to know what you're doing. First comes the little twinge, then the heat, and then more heat. If you do it right, it works every time. My procedure

The Star Patrol helmet. I've never been quite the same without it.

You looking for Johnstone?
Nope, haven't seen
him all day.

No, Garv, I didn't get traded. But with my
track record, it never hurts to be prepared.

Oh, the joy of being a Dodger (that's Rick Sutcliffe between Garvey and me).

I always thought it was a shame that baseball has no cheerleaders, so I did the honors at the USC-Dodgers exhibition game.

Penguin, Moon Man,
Davey Lopes, and Dave
"Wacko" Goltz celebrate
the 1981 Championship
(before somebody swiped
my Star Patrol helmet.)

The life of a pinch hitter:
standing around doing nothing,
trying to look cool.

That's my true love, Mary Jayne Sarah, in 1981. I'm just
telling those other ball players to keep their hands off.

I just hope we sound better on the record
than we look on the jacket.

Seriously, I never saw this woman before in my life. You think it's easy dealing with groupies?

If I can just get out of here before Tommy catches me. . . .

Bogie and I, just back from Casablanca.

The world's greatest fans.

Bring out the victory glasses and everybody wants to get in on the act
That's presidential press secretary James Brady.

Hey, for a free T-shirt, I'll plug anything.

I guess Leon hung around me a little too long.

It was a helluva lot easier with the batting tee.

JAY JOHNSTONE'S LIFETIME STATISTICS

YEAR	CLUB	AVG.	G	AB	R	H	2B	3B	HR	RBI	BB	SO	SB
1963	San Jose[1]	.252	48	155	21	39	5	3	1	18	10	45	3
1964	San Jose[1]	.291	126	454	66	132	27	11	4	48	39	81	13
1965	El Paso[1]	.285	35	137	21	39	9	2	1	21	13	11	1
	San Jose[1]	.301	97	356	53	107	17	6	6	60	26	21	9
1966	El Paso[1]	.360	7	25	5	9	2	0	1	1	3	3	0
	Seattle[1]	.340	81	318	60	108	14	7	7	42	16	31	11
	California Angels	.264	61	254	35	67	12	4	3	17	11	36	3
1967	California Angels	.209	79	230	18	48	7	1	2	10	5	37	3
	Seattle[1]	.315	49	184	21	58	11	1	4	21	7	17	2
1968	California Angels	.261	41	115	11	30	4	1	0	3	7	15	2
	Seattle[1]	.277	84	314	45	87	15	4	13	56	22	47	4
1969	California Angels	.270	148	540	64	146	20	5	10	59	38	75	3
1970	California Angels	.238	119	320	34	76	10	5	11	39	24	53	1
1971	Chicago White Sox	.260	124	388	53	101	14	1	16	40	38	50	10
1972	Chicago White Sox	.188	113	261	27	49	9	0	4	17	25	42	2
1973	Oakland A's	.107	23	28	1	3	1	0	0	3	2	4	0
1974	Tucson[2]	.347	69	242	58	84	15	5	9	44	30	26	4
	Toledo[3]	.316	57	155	31	49	15	1	8	25	24	25	2
	Philadelphia Phillies	.295	64	200	30	59	10	4	6	30	24	28	5

YEAR	CLUB	AVG.	G	AB	R	H	2B	3B	HR	RBI	BB	SO	SB
1975	Philadelphia Phillies	.329	122	350	50	115	19	2	7	54	42	39	7
1976	Philadelphia Phillies	.318	129	440	62	140	38	4	5	53	41	39	5
1977	Philadelphia Phillies	.284	112	363	64	103	18	4	15	59	38	38	3
1978	Philadelphia Phillies	.179	35	56	3	10	2	0	0	4	6	9	0
	New York Yankees	.262	36	65	6	17	0	0	1	6	4	10	0
1979	New York Yankees	.208	23	48	7	10	1	0	1	7	2	7	1
	San Diego Padres	.294	75	201	10	59	8	2	0	32	18	21	1
1980	Los Angeles Dodgers	.307	109	251	31	77	15	2	2	20	24	29	3
1981	Los Angeles Dodgers	.205	61	83	8	17	3	0	3	6	7	13	0
1982	Los Angeles Dodgers	.077	21	13	1	1	1	0	0	2	5	2	0
	Chicago Cubs	.249	98	269	39	67	13	1	10	43	40	41	0
1983	Chicago Cubs	.257	86	140	16	36	7	0	6	22	20	24	1
1984	Chicago Cubs	.288	52	73	8	21	2	2	0	3	7	18	0
	American League Totals	.243	767	2249	256	547	78	17	48	201	156	329	25
	National League Totals	.289	964	2439	322	705	136	21	54	328	372	301	25
	Major League Totals	.267	1731	4688	578	1252	214	38	102	529	428	630	50

[1]California Angels—minor league
[2]Oakland A's—minor league
[3]Philadelphia Phillies—minor league

Just glad to be here.

is a lot better than just flaring a match under a guy's foot. My style has slower action, and that's important.

Why? Because by the time the victim's foot gets hot, you're never around to get caught.

The biggest joke about umpires, of course, is their eyesight. It's no wonder that fans keep offering them their glasses. I've known umps who literally couldn't see.

I'll never forget the night Mary Jayne and I were having dinner at the Gene Autry Hotel in Palm Springs, California, where the Angels lived during spring training. We walked into the dining room, and there was umpire Emmett Ashford's head behind this huge, tall menu.

What we didn't know, of course, is that he couldn't read the menu without his glasses. He would never dream of wearing glasses during a game. He just went out and made the calls with his usual flamboyance, whether he saw the play or not.

So just as I walk over to his table he's taking out his bifocals to read the menu, and his face couldn't have been two inches from the bill of fare.

"Hey, Emmett, how ya' doin'?" I chirped, and he set a land-speed record for getting those glasses off his nose and into his vest pocket.

But what the hell. It was no big deal that Emmett needed glasses. He was the first black umpire in baseball and certainly one of the most dramatic. So what if he didn't always watch the play before calling a guy out? Emmett is dead now, and baseball has lost a funny, kind man.

I don't think I've been thrown out of games by umpires more than five times. I can live with that.

Once I got tossed for having white tape around my shoes. I was with the Dodgers in San Diego and had already pinch hit. So now I get thrown out? Figure that one out. I was already out of the game, anyhow.

Another time I asked for it, literally.

It was the last day of the season with the Angels, mid-1960s, and we're in Minnesota, Bill Haller is the first base umpire. And before the game, I say to him: "Hey, Bill, I got a plane to catch. Can you throw me out of this game early?"

"I can't do that," he says. "We just don't do things like that, Jay."

Now it's the third inning, and I'm on first base with a hit, and I turn to Haller and start screaming at him.

"Hey, that's a balk," I shout, referring to the pitcher.

"You're out of here," he says, and just like that I was gone.

Whoever said umpires aren't people?

Players and umpires have been shouting at each other, I would assume, since the Boston Red Stockings, Fort Wayne Kekiongas, New York Mutuals, Chicago White Stockings, and Rockford Forest Citys, among others, were in combat back in the 1870s, when baseball became a professional sport.

It has become part of the game's ritual.

Lou Boudreau, Hall of Fame shortstop and in recent years an announcer for the Chicago Cubs, illustrates the ritual of this "adversary" relationship between player and umpire:

"It was 1948, when I was player-manager for the Cleveland Indians," says Boudreau, "and we were playing one of those crucial doubleheaders in Yankee Stadium before about 65,000 people. I'm at shortstop, and the second base umpire, Art Passarella, had been having a bad day. There had been several close plays, and we'd had words on a couple of occasions.

"Now it's toward the end of the second game, and Art blows another one at second. I come running over and start to argue and as I yell 'Horseshit,' I lose my chewing gum.

" 'Have you got any chewing gum?' " I shout at him.

" 'Hell, no. I don't have any gum,' he shouts back. 'You think I carry gum around just for you?'

"Now I'm really mad, and I keep yelling and waving my arms, and our faces are about three inches apart.

" 'Well, you oughta have chewing gum because your breath smells,' I shout and now he's getting really mad, too. Then I point toward the third base umpire and yell, 'Has he got any gum?'

" 'How in hell should I know if he has any gum?' yells Passarella back and I mean we're really putting on a show. Both dugouts are screaming, and 65,000 are screaming because they thought I pointed to third base for an appeal play.

"I'll swear it's the truth. We must have argued for five minutes out there, and neither of us mentioned the play at second after I yelled, 'Horseshit,' and lost my chewing gum."

Everybody in an argument, of course, always wants to get in the last shot. The good ones are always remembered.

Pee Wee Reese, captain of Brooklyn's first world championship team in 1955 tells about a rapid but memorable confrontation with umpire George Magerkurth. The "Major" of course, was a giant of a man, and Reese was 5'10", 160 pounds.

During a difference of opinion, Magerkurth finally towered over Reese and said, "Get out of here or I'll bite your head off."

"If you do," snapped Pee Wee, "you'll have more brains in your stomach than you do in your head."

Reese and surviving teammates from that 1955 Brooklyn Dodgers championship team held a rare, 30-year reunion at the beginning of spring training, 1985, at Dodgertown, Vero Beach, Florida, guests of Dodger owner Peter O'Malley. Roy Campanella was there. So were Clem Labine, Billy Loes, Sandy Amoros, Carl Erskine, Carl Furillo, Sandy Koufax (a rookie in 1955), and most of the others.

There was a lot of nostalgia, of course, and certainly some sober moments as they mourned deceased team-mates such as Jackie Robinson, Gil Hodges, Karl Spooner, Jim Gilliam, and the 1955 manager, Walter Alston.

There were also a lot of laughs, as those Dodgers of the mid-'50s recalled their special camaraderie ("It wasn't unusual for 15 of us to show up at the same place for dinner," said Reese) and occasional hijinks.

My favorite story comes from Russ (Mad Monk) Meyer, who won 15 games for the Dodgers in 1953 and a half-dozen when they won the World Series in 1955.

It's the story about how hot-tempered Meyer, also known as "Russell the Red-Necked Reindeer," ended up with a resin bag on his head. Monk tells it this way:

"I had just been traded from the Phillies to the Dodgers in 1953, and it was my first start against my old club. You might say I was charged up. And I was pitching a good game, too—it was close, 1–1, bottom of the eighth—and Augie Donatelli, the home plate umpire, had been squeezing the strike zone on me all day.

"Now Philly gets the bases loaded, and I throw a 3–2 curve ball to Richie Ashburn. But he bows to it, and Augie calls it a ball. Hell, Campy was so sure it was a strike he had already rolled the ball back to the mound. It was one of the few times I ever saw Campanella upset.

"And me, well, I'm bananas. I charge Augie and call him a 'fuckin' homer,' and the next thing you know, he tosses me.

"Except that I won't go. I won't leave the mound. Our manager, Charlie Dressen, comes out and I say, 'Fuck you, too, I ain't leavin'.' I'm out there stompin' and shoutin', and nobody can get me off the mound. Finally, though, Augie figures it out. He comes out and threatens to fine me more money if I don't leave.

"So I figure 'the hell with it' and start walking off the mound. But somehow I still had the resin bag in my hand, so I just fire it underhanded into the air and keep on walking. Well, I must have taken six or seven full strides, so help me, when that resin bag comes down and hits me smack in the middle of the head and sticks there. You couldn't have done it in a million years if you tried. Even I broke up.

"But by the time I got to the dugout I was mad again and wouldn't leave. I'm standing there at the corner of the dugout in Old Shibe Park, and I'm still giving it to Augie, so he comes over after me.

"That's when I grabbed my crotch and gave him a salute. But what I didn't know was that this was a nationally televised game and I was on candid camera. They caught me in the act. Well, TV was just beginning then with baseball, and the commissioner, Ford Frick, got so shook up that he sent out a memo the following week, prohibiting any camera shots of players in the dugout.

"I always called it the Monk Meyer Rule, but nobody follows it anymore."

Meyer and Reese, incidentally, are still fierce competitors. During their Dodgertown reunion, they got into an argument over who could swim the fastest to the other end of the pool.

There they were, fully clothed, poised at the end of the swimming pool, ready for action—Reese, age 66, and Meyer, age 61, one-time teammates and forever competitors. It took Tom Lasorda and a group of wives to talk them out of their challenge swim.

Boys of Summer, one supposes, will always be boys.

And, sometimes, the boys who play baseball can be *bad* boys. Take Reggie Smith for example.

Reggie Smith has managed to get into quite a few skirmishes during his career. Maybe it was his attitude. Like the time he and Pascual Perez, then with the Pirates, challenged each other to meet in the tunnel between locker rooms behind home plate.

"You threw at one of our guys," yells Reggie.

"I see you back there," yells Perez, pointing toward the tunnel, and even though I'm standing next to Reggie, I figure it's all just hot air.

Now the inning is over, and I'll be damned if Perez doesn't throw his glove and take off for the tunnel through the Pittsburgh dugout. And here goes Reggie through our dugout.

Players from both teams follow, of course, and the next thing you know, we've got the biggest traffic jam in the history of Pennsylvania. The funny part is that the tunnel guard was sitting there in a chair, dozing, and all of a sudden he's in a crush. You can hear spikes scraping and guys yelling and cussin', and nobody has any damned idea what he's gonna do.

One thing I do remember. The longer I looked at that Pittsburgh end of the tunnel, the bigger and blacker it got. There was Willie Stargell and Dave Parker and Jim Bibby and John Candelaria, and there's Bill Robinson, holding Perez, who's holding a bat in his hand. Christ, you'd have thought we were gonna fight the Harlem Globetrotters, and I'm saying to myself, "What am I doing here?"

So I just ease my back against the wall and observe the face-to-face macho stuff. Nobody gets hit, of course. Baseball players almost never hit or get hit. They just talk, push, and shove a lot. But it took a while to break this one up because the tunnel was so crowded the umpires couldn't get through. I think it was Danny Ozark, then a coach with the Dodgers, who got there in time to settle things down. If he hadn't gotten there maybe somebody could have gotten hurt. But not by me.

The only time I personally got in trouble happened in the stands, not on the field. In fact, the trouble is still pending.

I was with the Dodgers in San Francisco, and, in a way, Lasorda was the instigator. There was this old guy, maybe 90 years old, standing beside our dugout selling peanuts.

So Reggie Smith and I are standing there at the end of the dugout, and when Lasorda came our way Reggie says, "Hey, Tommy, there's a guy up here who says he once played baseball with you."

Well, Lasorda takes a look around the end of the dugout and sees this 90-year-old guy. I don't want to repeat what he said. But Reggie won't leave it alone. He yells up to the peanut vendor: "Didn't you once play baseball with Tom Lasorda?"

"Whattaya talkin' about?" the guy says. "Wanna buy some peanuts?"

Now some kids who had been drinking beer, and I mean a lot of beer, start yelling, "Hey, leave the guy alone," to Reggie.

From there, it's all downhill. Reggie is yelling into the stands, and they're yelling at him. And I walk past Lasorda and say, "See what you started?"

"Well," says Tommy, "you'd better go get some security."

So I get this security guard, but by the time the two of us get back to the other end of the dugout, all hell is breaking loose. There's a drunk running down the aisle toward Reggie, and he's got a number of well-oiled friends with him.

"Come on up here," the guy yells to Reggie.

"I can't come up," says Smith, "Why don't you come down here? Then we'll settle it."

Back and forth they go until the Giant fan finally says to Reggie: "What will it take to get you up here? What if I take off this helmet and throw it at you?"

"That just might do it," says Reggie, and just then, the guy whips off his fans' batting helmet and fires it into Reggie's hip.

Reggie is over the railing in a split second, and all I can say is, "Oh, shit."

It's chaos. Reggie is going one way, and the guy is coming from the other way, and there's got to be eight people in between them. The guy is in the second row, and the security guard, who isn't sure what he can do, is starting toward them.

Enter Jay Johnstone, peacemaker. I go over the railing to join the security guard because I can see three other buddies of this guy starting to move toward Reggie. And just as the loudmouth and Reggie start to square off, one of the buddies takes a roundhouse swing at Reggie and just misses.

Now I jump into the gang and start pushing people back—so help me, just trying to be Wyatt Earp. And just as it looks like everything is going to be OK, I look up and see this big black guy with glasses running down the aisle at high speed.

And just as he gets there, arms flailing, I grab one of the arms and throw him back about three rows. His glasses fly off, and he's out of the fight before he gets there.

It was Reggie Smith's cousin. He had just come to help. The reason I know is that afterward, in the clubhouse, this guy points a finger at me and says, "That's the guy!"

The whole scene was so crazy that I was so far up into the stands that the umpires didn't even see me. It's automatic ejection if you go into the audience, but they didn't throw me out.

We all got sued, of course. Lasorda, Smith, Davey Lopes, and I are named in the suit, but there's a motion to get me dismissed because videotapes show me up there pushing people away. Reggie was fined $5,000 by the league and $50 by the Dodgers. The suit was for $5,000,000. The guy who started it claimed he had a broken left hand and three broken ribs. Actually, he should thank me instead of suing me. The cops were beating on him so badly I was even trying to hold them off.

Who was it that said, "You can't beat fun at the old ballpark?" I'm here to tell you that you can if you've got a club.

Sometimes I wonder if all ball players should be equipped with clubs when they play in Candlestick Park in San Francisco.

It's a rough audience, especially when the Dodgers come into town. I haven't figured out yet who San Franciscans hate the most—the people who built that frigid mausoleum or the Dodgers.

It's my least-favorite ballpark in America.

My favorite? That's easy. You'll find it at the corner of Clark and Addison Streets on Chicago's north side.

Some of my favorite times in Chicago were spent sitting in the Wrigley Field bleachers when the other team was taking batting practice.

I loved being with the die-hard Cub fans, and nobody can tell me fans are more loyal anywhere else. Let's face it. We're playing baseball games for the fans. I'm sorry to say that a lot of ball players seem to have forgotten that. They've also forgotten that they wouldn't be getting paid if it weren't for the fans.

Baseball is an act. It's vaudeville. The players are showmen, and the diamond is our stage. I really believe that. What we do provides entertainment for millions of people. They can vent their frustrations, cry, laugh, scream, whatever they feel like doing. Even live out their fantasies. And we're damned lucky to have them buying tickets.

As a Cub, I got crazy once (just once) and bought 3,000 copies of a book called *Cub Mania*, written by Bob Ibach, the Cubs' publicist. It was my only venture into the book business until now. My idea was to sell the books to fans at a slightly higher price than I purchased them, and donate the proceeds to the fight against Lou Gehrig's disease. Frankly, I don't know if I made any money at all, but I sure met a lot of new and interesting people. I'd take the books into the stands with me—in full uniform, of course—and mingle.

First, though, we had to solve a little problem. When the

publisher delivered the books, I wasn't there, and the truck driver didn't know where to leave them. So I told Ibach on the phone, "Just put them in my locker." Can you imagine 3,000 books in a locker? Clubhouse man Yosh Kawano almost shot me. We finally stored them in WGN television's helicopter hangar, and everytime I'd need a new supply, I'd visit the hangar for another boxful.

Sometimes, too, I'd lead cheers—left-field bleachers against right-field bleachers. That doesn't make me original in Chicago. They tell me Dick Selma was doing it with a towel from the bullpen back in 1969. But I'll tell you this: He couldn't have gotten more enthusiasm from the fans than we got in 1984 en route to that divisional title.

It's a cliché but true. Chicago baseball fans are behind their teams 110 percent. New York fans are slightly more knowledgeable. Philadelphia fans love to boo. California fans? They're laid back, sometimes way back.

But fans are fans, no matter where you go, and remember, the word came from *fanatic.*

I'd never seen anything like Cub fans when I first went to Chicago. Sure, I'd visited Wrigley Field with the Phillies and Dodgers—and certainly we'd had plenty of fan enthusiasm for winning teams back home in Philadelphia and Los Angeles. But Cubs fans are a different breed. That's not just a creation of WGN television and Harry Caray. Cubs fans were that way long before cable systems started showing Cubs games to the rest of the nation. Real Cub fans love the Cubs, win or lose.

Attendance figures will show they always didn't go to the ballpark for losses, but the love was there. That's why when the Cubs finally did start winning, it seemed like new fans came crawling out from under rocks. Actually, they were there all the time. You don't need night baseball to break attendance records on the north side of Chicago. You just need a winner.

The thing I always loved about Cub fans (at least, when

I was a Cub) was how they wouldn't tolerate visiting teams. The Bleacher Bums buried them. They buried the umpires. They buried anything but their beloved Cubs. I have to wonder how the personality of the bleachers will change now that the Cubs' management is selling bleacher seats in advance. Does that mean the left- and right-field seats will be filled with yuppies with corporation tickets if the Cubs are fighting again for a pennant? I don't like the new policy, but it's not my business. Still, I can't believe the Bleacher Bums like it.

Something else about Chicago baseball fans: If a man tells you he's a fan of both the Sox and the Cubs, check your wallet, make sure your watch is still on your wrist, and lock your car doors. It doesn't work that way in Chicago. You're a Cub fan or a Sox fan. It's OK to hope the other guy does well once in a while, but being a fan of both? Not in a city where the love of baseball teams runs that deep.

When I played in Comiskey Park in the early 1970s, Sox fans were drunker and rowdier than they have been under new management. I remember how they tore out all the seats once and started throwing them onto the field. They're more civilized now, but it's still a blue-collar crowd and still very loyal to the south siders. Yet, I don't think that loyalty is quite as fervent as you'll find in Wrigley Field. Maybe it's just because the Cubs haven't been in a World Series since 1945, one year before I was born.

About that subject: There has been a discrepancy about my age. I was born on November 20, 1946, in Manchester, Connecticut, home of the Manchester Nutmeggers. Yet, somewhere along the line, several official baseball books started listing my birth date as 1945.

Frankly, I never bothered to correct the mistake. Then I

started noticing that people were listing me as 39 when I was only 38. And when a baseball player is approaching 40, he starts to pay more attention. I think the first mistake was made by the Topps people on a baseball card. Anyhow, I showed up for spring training, 1985, with a copy of my birth certificate. The record is now straight.

But I did have a few laughs with the age mistake along the way. Bob Verdi, sports columnist for the *Chicago Tribune*, once pointed to 1945 in some official baseball book.

"But the book doesn't know I spent one year in Australia," I said.

"Oh," said Verdi.

Back to fans: In New York they will amaze you with their knowledge of the game. If you get a runner over to the next base, even though you make an out, they know when to applaud. Cubs fans loved you whether you got the guy over or not. Yankee fans, though, were really aware of game situations. You might get a little whiff of funny smoke from the crowd once in a while, but there was always an excitement about a Yankee Stadium audience. And talk about a deafening roar? No ball player can deny the excitement of playing in Yankee Stadium.

In Philly, well, I don't want to call the fans vicious, but they do boo just to boo. They don't care what you do. They still boo. They really do love the Phillies, but if the ball game was rained out, they'd all go down to the airport and boo landings.

We were in the midst of a 13-game winning streak back in August 1976, and we were six games on top. It was the fourth inning, and Dave Cash made an error. Then Larry Bowa made an error. Atlanta got four runs, and as we ran off the field, they started booing us. We'd won 11 in a row on the way to a pennant, and they were booing.

Manager Ozark would go to the mound, and they'd boo.

So he put his jacket on Ray Ripplemeyer, the pitching coach, and sent *him* to the mound. If Ray went out without a jacket, it was OK. But if he wore Danny's jacket, he got booed.

Yet these were the same fans who gave me some of my greatest thrills, calling me back for encores after I did something good at the plate. And still, to this day, when I go back to Veterans Stadium in Philadelphia I receive an ovation. But nobody can boo like Phillies fans. Nobody.

And how about Dodger fans? It's more like, "Here I am at the game. Hi, how's my hair? Hi, how are you? Still working on that script? Oh, you did your nails today. Nice."

You really do see celebrities in the audience at a Dodger game. You also see a lot of people who go to be seen. People love sports in southern California, but if it isn't a Dodger game, it's a horse race, or a basketball game. There is always something. I mean they "dress" for games.

And when it's the seventh or eighth inning, look out. It's a mad rush for the parking lot. It's even worse in Anaheim for Angel games. I've never understood, because both stadiums are among the best in the world for cars to exit. Maybe Dodger fans just want to get into their cars to listen to Vin Scully. Or, more than likely, they've had their evening of entertainment and want to go home. The score? Gee, I hope the Dodgers won.

I'm not saying Dodger fans aren't loyal. They're just different. You don't see Dodger fans carrying lunches. Some of them don't even want to throw peanut shells on the floor. It's the cleanest stadium in America and they don't want to mess it up. Yet, all fans will fool you at certain times. Back in 1980 when we won those final three games of the season at home against Houston to force a playoff, Dodger fans were fantastic—on their feet from start to finish. It was one time I really felt they caught fire.

A similar thing happened last October in San Diego when the Padres, after losing two in a row, came back to beat the Cubs in the NL playoffs. I couldn't believe San Diego fans. I was awestruck because, remember, I'd played there in 1979 and, frankly, I thought the whole town was asleep or waiting for the next aircraft carrier. But last October I'm standing in the tunnel, thinking to myself: "I hope to hell our guys [the Cubs] don't let this get to them." I was really thrilled to hear it and felt like it was experiencing a part of baseball history. An entire city had awakened.

Ball players, incidentally, should always be careful about what they say about cities unless they're prepared to hear themselves booed, or worse. Once with the Yankees I was interviewed on the "NBC Game of the Week," and I said, "I drove through Cleveland one day, but it was closed." The next thing I knew, the mayor of Cleveland called NBC and demanded an apology.

He didn't get it, but boy, did I get it the next time I played in Cleveland.

66

Fernando earns more than $1 million a year, and that's just for throwing baseballs. He also does commercials for television. Frankly, I always thought he would have been perfect as the Pillsbury Dough Boy, if only he could have laughed in English.

99

8

DID BABE RUTH REALLY COME BACK AS A MEXICAN?

"On our first date, Jay got up during the movie to get popcorn. He didn't come back for twenty minutes, and he was panting.
" 'Sorry,' he says, 'they were out of popcorn here. I had to run down the block to another theatre.' "

Mary Jayne Johnstone

I have never met a left-handed Mexican pitcher I didn't like.

They make me laugh. Don't ask me why; they just do. I look at a southpaw Mex, and I start thinking about burritos, tacos, and screwballs.

Have you ever looked real closely at Fernando Valenzuela, the señor who was born in Sonora, Mexico, in 1960, and stood the baseball world on its enchilada when he pitched for the Dodgers in 1981? Look real closely next time. That really isn't Fernando Valenzuela at all. It's Babe Ruth playing a joke on all of us. He came back as a Mexican.

Find an old picture of Babe Ruth and take a good look. Full face, sneaky smile, pokable tummy. The Bambino was a pitcher first, wasn't he? Fernando is a good hitter, isn't he? Somewhere in time, these two lefties became one.

Except that I don't think Babe Ruth ever made funny faces like Fernando. It may have started when Freddy (his nickname with the Dodgers), who, unable to speak English when he first came up, used his face to express ideas and emotions to his teammates.

Now he does speak English—not fluently, but with improvement every day, it seems—but he still makes faces, sometimes like a little kid at the back of the room in first grade.

A couple of years ago at Wrigley Field, in fact, it got him into trouble. The game between the Cubs and Dodgers had been delayed by the home plate umpire, who insisted that Fernando return to the Dodger clubhouse and remove the flaps on his shoes, which had been painted white. Hitters were complaining, said the ump, that the white flaps were a distraction.

More accurately, it was Fernando's screwball that was the distraction, but there was no way to get rid of it. So Freddy went into the clubhouse, got rid of the white flaps, and came back. And you could see he wasn't very happy.

Now, about two pitches later, the home plate umpire is standing off to the side of home plate, glaring at Fernando.

"Whattaya looking at my pitcher like that for?" shouted Dodger manager Tom Lasorda from the dugout.

"Because I don't like the way he looks," said the umpire.

"What's wrong with the way he looks?" yelled back Lasorda.

"He keeps making faces at me," said the umpire, "I don't like that face."

At which time Lasorda, who was also boiling mad, pointed toward Ron Cey of the Cubs, who was standing in the batting circle.

"How can you talk about my pitcher's face when that guy has an ugly face like that?" screamed Lasorda.

Valenzuela, from the beginning, showed that he had a

sense of humor. Unable to communicate with words, he would slip up behind teammates and use the oldest trick in memory—tap somebody on one shoulder, then go to the other side where he wouldn't be seen at first glance. It was his way of letting you know he liked you, of saying, "Hi, friend . . . hi."

Fernando earns more than $1 million a year now, and that's just for throwing baseballs. He also does commercials for television. Frankly, I always thought he would have been perfect as the Pillsbury Dough Boy, if only he could have laughed in English.

Two stories about Fernando's use of his limited vocabulary in English:

The first comes from Lasorda, who speaks fluent Spanish after all of his years of managing during the off-season in winter ball.

Fernando was pitching one day and getting shelled in the first innning. He's a lot like Warren Spahn and Sandy Koufax in that respect. If you're going to get to Freddy, get to him early.

Anyhow, three runs are in, and Lasorda runs to the mound. He starts lecturing Valenzuela in Spanish.

"Just hold them to three runs now," said Lasorda, "and we'll win this game. Three runs are nothing. Just don't give them any more, understand?"

Valenzuela shuffled his feet, nodded his head, and prepared to pitch.

But Lasorda wasn't satisfied. Once again, in Spanish, he resumed his lecture.

"I'm telling you Fernando, that if you stop them right now—no more runs—we will win this game. No more runs. Stop them right now. We will win."

This time Valenzuela looked Lasorda directly in the eye and said, in perfect English: "Are you sure?"

Story number two about Spanish-speaking Valenzuela: During spring training, 1985, National League umpiring supervisor Ed Vargo was touring Grapefruit League camps to offer routine demonstrations on current balk rule interpretation.

Vargo, former umpire, was surrounded on a practice mound by Dodgers pitchers and coaches. And as he would show various "dos" and "don'ts" of pitching, he would talk to the players by name.

Vargo, however, doesn't do very well with names. He kept calling instructor Maury Wills "Murray," and every time he addressed Valenzuela, he'd call him "Orlando."

And every time Vargo would say "Orlando," Fernando would make a face and Rick Honeycutt would laugh.

Finally, Valenzuela stepped forward, held up his hand, and said to Vargo, "I'm not Orlando. I'm Tampa."

Fernando isn't the first to prove a pitcher doesn't have to speak the language to get his point across on the mound. Consider the case of Masanori Murakami, the pride of Otsuki, Japan, who pitched for the San Francisco Giants in 1964 and 1965.

Murakami, a southpaw, compiled a career 5–1 record with nine saves and a 3.43 ERA coming out of the bullpen for manager Herman Franks. But, realizing that Murakami couldn't speak a word of English, his caring teammates from the bullpen decided to help. They took him aside and painstakingly taught him what to say the next time Franks visited the mound.

And sure enough, the next time Franks strolled from the dugout, Murakami looked him in the eye and said, "Take a hike."

Franks was dumbfounded, and Masanori didn't even know what he had said.

Henry Aguirre, the only other 100-percent left-handed Mexican pitcher I've ever known, had no trouble with the English language.

Hank, who pitched from 1955 through 1970 with the Cleveland Indians, Detroit Tigers, Los Angeles Dodgers, and Chicago Cubs, was born in Azusa, California, and grew up in San Gabriel. Both of his parents came from Mexico, but Hank was just another American kid.

He spent 10 years of his career with the Tigers, who trained in what was then "remote" Lakeland, Florida, and his running mate in those days was another pitcher and celebrated Yankee killer, Frank (Taters) Lary.

One night Aguirre and Lary decided to steal a Greyhound bus.

They had wearied of rigging the pinball machine at the local Elks Club (Larry had placed a magnet in the machine) and when wandering outside at 1:00 A.M. (closing time) they spotted the bus parked across the street.

"Actually, we didn't want to go very far," Aguirre recalled. "But we wanted one more drink, and the only place open was an AmVets Club, and we didn't have any wheels. Just a couple of friendly guys looking for a ride, that's all."

The two pitchers were accompanied by three other Tiger players—George Thomas, Chuck Cottier, and Bobo Osborne—and perhaps one or two female companions, and all felt that the appropriation of the bus for transportation to the next saloon was in order.

There were two problems, however. One, they couldn't get it started. Two, it had been chartered by the Fordham Rowing Crew, in Florida for competition, and the collegians, awakened in their hotel by noise, came outside to investigate.

One setback led to another and soon there was a free-for-all brawl going on inside the bus—five baseball players wrestling the collegians, who were now dedicated to saving their bus.

"I think what made us maddest was their coach," said Aguirre. "He was wearing one of those blazers with an Olympic emblem on it, and he kept calling us 'nasty pros.' "

The prowling Tigers had made one other miscalculation. The bus was parked in front of the Lakeland police station. Soon the cops were also involved, and it was a genuine three-ring circus. No charges were filed, however; the bus was cleared; and the players found another ride to their next watering hole.

Aguirre, though, wouldn't leave it alone. At 3:00 A.M. he picked up the phone, called the stuffed-shirt coach from Fordham, and shouted, "Don't go to sleep because we're still going to steal your bus."

The coach reciprocated by phoning Tigers manager Bob Scheffing at 3:15 A.M. to complain about his team's threat to take the Fordham bus.

"Let them have it," said Scheffing, and went back to sleep.

Aguirre is now a successful businessman in Detroit, owner of Mexican Industries in Michigan, Inc., and employer of 126 people, of which 110 are Hispanic.

And when he speaks at banquets, he always tells the story about his first day as a major leaguer. It was memorable, indeed.

The lanky, 6'4", 210-pound Aguirre, you see, had never even seen a major league ballpark before the Indians called him up in 1955. Cleveland, however, was fighting for a pennant with the Yankees and desperately needed another left-handed pitcher out of the bullpen.

Aguirre's first day with the club was in Boston, and the game was on national television. And sure enough, in the bottom of the fifth Hank was called in to face the great Ted Williams.

"I struck him out on three pitches," says Aguirre. "And the next inning Ralph Kiner hit a grand slam for us and we won the game. I had faced only one hitter, but got the victory.

"So afterward, I was real excited. In one day I had seen

my first major league park, struck out Ted Williams, appeared on national TV, and gotten credit for a victory.

Young Aguirre was so thrilled that he even took the baseball with which he had whiffed Williams into the enemy clubhouse, shyly asking the great hitter to autograph it. Williams complied.

Two weeks later, however, the Red Sox came into Cleveland—and, inasmuch as Aguirre had enjoyed so much success against Williams before, he was called into the game to face him again.

Williams lined Henry's first pitch inside the right-field foul pole for a giant home run. And as the Thumper jogged around first base, he yelled toward Aguirre: "Hey, kid, go get that ball and I'll sign it, too."

Aguirre was an expert on great hitters because he was one of the worst hitters. His career pitching record was 75–72, but his career batting average was .085.

"I thought hitting .333 was one hit in three years," Aguirre would say. Actually, he had 33 lifetime hits in 388 at bats, and in 1962 went 2 for 75.

He remembers all 33 hits, especially the triple in 1967:

"Big game against the Yankees. I was the starting pitcher, second game of a doubleheader, and in the second inning we've got runners on second and third. So [Yankee manager] Ralph Houk intentionally walks Ray Oyler to get to me.

"Fritz Peterson gets two quick strikes on me, and I figure, for sure, that he's now gonna come with a curve. But Ellie Howard is the catcher, and he's guessing what I'm guessing and calls for another fastball.

"Well, Fritz threw it right where I swung, and I hit it over Joe Pepitone's head to the 401 mark in right center field. One hop. Three runs score, and I slide into third base, one of those perfect pop-up slides. Guys in my dugout are applauding.

"Now I'm on third, and Peterson doesn't even look at me

when he makes his first pitch. I mean I was halfway to home plate. Same with the next pitch. He's so mad he's ignoring me like I wasn't even on third base.

"So now I go back to third base coach Tony Cuccinello and say, "Hey, Tony, I think I can steal home."

"And Tony says, 'Hank, you got this far . . . don't fuck it up.' "

Final anecdote from Henry John Aguirre—and it demonstrates, once again, the differences between ballplayers of yesterday and today:

"I was with the Tigers, and we'd had a long flight to Anaheim to play the Angels. And as our bus pulled up to the Grand Hotel across from Disneyland, somebody noticed that a Chinese Art Exposition was being held at the hotel.

"And parked right in front of the hotel was this beautiful Flying Tigers airplane, the old P-51s, right? Immediately Jerry Lumpe says, "We gotta fly that SOB. We're the Flying Tigers, aren't we?"

"So we start planning. I mean it becomes a team project, right down to synchronizing our watches. We're gonna get that airplane before we get out of town. It's a caper that has everybody on the team excited.

"Finally, after the final game of the three-game series, 17 of us go up to Norm Cash's room for a few drinks and final planning. We were gonna wait until midnight, but we were so anxious we couldn't wait. Somebody said, 'Let's go get it,' and we raced for the elevator.

"I get into the cockpit, and the other 16 guys start pushing me up and down the street. Then we tired of that, and somebody said, 'Let's put it into the swimming pool.' But there was a wire fence around the pool, and we couldn't do that.

"Finally, with me still in the cockpit acting like the Red Baron, they pushed the nose of the plane right into the front entrance of the hotel. Then we all went upstairs to Cash's room.

"But a little later the hotel manager calls and says, 'Boys, I think you'd better move that plane.'

" 'What plane?' said Cash.

" 'OK,' said the hotel boss, 'I'm going to have to call your manager.'

"Well, our manager was Frank Skaff, and a few minutes later he calls to say, 'Norm, move that airplane.'

"So three of us go downstairs about 2:00 A.M.—Dick McAuliffe, Cash, and me, the pilot—and there's Skaff standing there looking at his wristwatch. Understand now, that 16 guys had pushed that plane almost into the lobby, but now we've got only three guys trying to push it away. And we weren't in the best of shape either.

"Finally, I look at Skaff standing there, and I said, 'Frank, don't look at your watch. Just help us push.' "

Helping push, I guess, is the point. There were 17 Tigers of a 25-man roster in that hotel room that night, plotting the silliness of pushing an airplane with a Mexican pilot down an Anaheim street.

"There was a closeness among the players that I don't see today," said Aguirre, and he's right. He doesn't see it because it isn't there. If 17 players get together nowadays, it's usually just to vote on something that will bring them more money.

Maybe I'm just getting old. How come nobody steals buses or airplanes anymore? And how come nobody tries to pick a man off first base while playing right field?

That's right, right field. If you're scoring at home, make that a 2–9 putout.

For neophytes, that means the catcher threw a baseball to the rightfielder, who tagged out the base runner.

I was the rightfielder, and to my knowledge, it's the only time the play has ever been made in major league baseball history.

Hey, it's a sandlot play. The rightfielder is supposed to catch fly balls, not pick guys off first base. But I've always had one philosophy about defense: You cheat, lie, steal or do anything you can to get the other guy out.

Principal characters in our historic 2–9 pickoff: Johnny Oates was the Phillies catcher, Dick Allen was at first base, Dave Cash at second, I was in right field, and Frank Taveras of the Pirates was the base runner.

Bruce Kison was the hitter, and he was trying to sacrifice bunt. Allen was charging the bunt, and because second baseman Cash was so far away, Taveras figured he could take a giant lead.

But he forgot about me. So did the Pittsburgh first base coach, Jose Pagan. Taveras was watching the first baseman, Pagan was watching the second baseman, and nobody was watching me except Oates, who wasn't sure he could believe what he was seeing.

He's seeing this wild-eyed rightfielder running full-speed toward first base. Naturally, he reacts. His throw hit me in full stride at first base, and Taveras was a dead duck. It took the Bucs out of an inning and helped us win an important game.

It's crazy, this thing about me and defense. In all the years I spent in the American League, it was "great defense, work on your hitting." I played great defensive center field. Then I got into the National League, and it was "great hitting, work on your defense," as if I'd never worn a glove.

Actually, I could have been playing center field during much of my career in the NL. But when I got to Philly, they had Garry Maddox, so I played right. Then I went to the Yankees, and they had Mickey Rivers, so when I played I was in left. Finally, I got to play center in San Diego.

But after I once misjudged a fly ball in Los Angeles, Al Campanis got down on me and decided I couldn't play outfield anymore.

Then I went to Chicago in 1982, and Dallas Green asked me if I could play defense.

"You haven't been out there in a year and a half," he said.

"Just give me a glove."

And I played hellacious defense for the Cubs. Everybody was amazed. I must have run into one brick wall three times in one game at Wrigley Field. After the last time, I just lay there dazed. One of our players' mothers said after the game: "Why does the pitcher keep making that poor boy out there run into the wall?"

There is no more difficult outfield to play than Wrigley Field. Right field is easier than left (although Lou Brock might not agree) in Chicago because at least you can see the ball coming off the bat. But in left, the field slopes in such a manner that you can lose the ball in the background. You have to crouch down almost to the ground to pick up the ball.

There are also other factors in Chicago—sun, wind, brick walls, metal grates in which you can get your cleats stuck, curvature of the wall, and that ivy that has a way of devouring baseballs. It does make baseball fun.

Piersall taught me to cheat according to the hitter and pitcher. It's a basic premise of good outfield play.

Example: If you have a right-field hitter and a left-handed sinker-ball pitcher, chances are the hitter won't pull the ball. He's going to go with the pitch, so you cheat two or three steps.

Example: If Fergie Jenkins is pitching and there's a power, pull hitter at the plate, remember that Fergie doesn't throw that hard anymore and he may hang one of his off-speed pitches. Figure, then, he'll pull the ball, and you cheat in that direction.

You move on every pitch because every ball-strike count may create a different situation.

Example: With two strikes on the first, second, sixth, seventh, or eighth hitters in the lineup, you can usually move in 10 steps because they're trying to protect the plate.

Example: If you see a right-handed hitter fouling off balls toward first base, he's late so you cheat.

Example: On 2 and 0, the hitter is looking for something he can juice. On 3 and 0, 3 and 1, even 3 and 2, the good hitters are still looking for it—but those first, second, sixth, seventh, and eighth hitters are just trying to protect the plate. On 0 and 2 they're choking up, just trying for contact. Every count situation is different. That's how I was brought up in baseball.

When pitchers are hitting, remember this: 90 percent of them can't hit the ball over your head. And 90 percent of the pitchers who bunt will miss the first pitch.

One should not surmise, however, that I have always been perfect in the outfield. Once in San Francisco I lost a pop fly in the sun. I brought down the sunglasses, but I was still running around like a puppet on a string. Finally I had to dive for the ball, and I grabbed it as my elbows dug into the grass and my glasses flopped across my face. Then the ball came out. They ran a three-page photo sequence of it the next day in the newspaper.

Once too, when with the Angels, I was playing left field in Yankee Stadium, and I went racing after a rocket off the bat of Elston Howard. I flipped back my glasses to catch the ball, but as I did, they broke and I missed the ball. Actually, I wasn't even close.

Bill Rigney wanted to kill me for that one, but in the same game I went against the fence and somehow caught a ball behind my back.

Some guys provide adventure in the outfield. Like Jerry Turner. He played left field in San Diego when I was in center, and he almost killed me one night.

There were runners on first and second, and a ball is hit into the left-center-field gap. I'm in center. I race over and start to go into this sliding dive to catch the ball, but Turner cuts in front of me and catches it.

Remember, now. Runners on first and second. I'm sliding one way toward the left-field foul line, and he's running the other way, toward center, with the ball.

But as he tries to whirl and throw to second, he slips and fires the ball past my head. It narrowly misses me and goes down into the bullpen in the left-field corner. Everybody is running, everybody is scoring, and I'm just happy to be alive.

But I love playing defense, even if some people have forgotten it was once my forte. I suppose I should have realized that once I became labeled as a hitter, then a pinch hitter at age 38, my days in the outfield would be limited.

They could, however, treat me with a little more respect. Once in 1982 I remember going to Lasorda and saying, "Monty [Coach Basgall] says he's going to use me for defensive purposes."

Replied Lasorda: "Was that Monty Hall?"

Also, I can remember when every pitching staff had maybe two guys who could really bring it, then two or three others whom you figured to hit. You would study the newspaper box scores to see how you might fatten up your average in a certain city. But now? They've got relief pitchers for every inning.

There were some pitching staff exceptions. Like when I broke in with the Angels, we'd go into Cleveland and it really didn't matter who was pitching. They were all killers—Sudden Sam McDowell, Gary Bell, Steve Hargan, Sonny Siebert, all throwing 90 miles an hour—then you might have to face Luis Tiant, who was no slouch.

Nowadays, however, I'm positive that the quality and variety of relief pitching has made a difference in home run production. If you hit 25 home runs today, you're a power hitter. Before, 20 home runs were nothing.

So I might as well surrender. They've got other bodies to put into the outfields of America. My job is to hit. Pinch hit, actually, and it's not a job for the fainthearted.

Frankly, pitching in the major leagues has become so specialized that it's a wonder anybody gets a hit anymore. I'm not kidding. Have you noticed the home run totals over the last five years? I'm not saying the pitchers are getting any better—just more specialized.

It's a rare day when a hitter faces a pitcher four times. More often, a hitter will face three or four different pitchers in four at-bats, and over the long haul, that does make a difference in batting averages.

Ted Williams always talked about how he liked to run a pitcher to a 3 and 2 count the first time up. By then, Ted figured he had seen all of his pitches and could adjust, accordingly, for the rest of the game. But nowadays that might be the only time you see the guy.

Ted Williams is the man who always said that hitting a baseball was the toughest thing in sports. And I'm a disciple who says that hitting a baseball when you're coming off the bench, bottom of the ninth, against somebody throwing heat or split-fingered magic, is the toughest part of the toughest thing.

But it's still better than lifting things.

"

The first time I met Moe Drabowsky was at one of Larry McTague's restaurants in New York, and Larry said, "Jay, I'd like you to meet Moe Drabowsky."

With that, Moe dropped his cocktail glass and reached out to shake my hand. I mean, it shattered all over the floor and he didn't blink an eye. I knew right away that this was my kind of guy.

"

CHAPTER
9
HOW LEGENDS LIVE ON
OR SCREAMING YELLOW, PHANTOM GREEN, AND THE PAINTED HORSE OF CHICAGO

"He is a genuine, gold-plated menace."

Rick Monday

Some things you plan, some you don't.

For example, I did not plan on nailing Svengoolie into his coffin. It just worked out that way.

Surely there was a full Chicago moon that night in the early 1970s, or maybe it was just the ridiculous situation in which I found myself.

Svengoolie was one of those Elvira types, a television personality who would introduce the late-late night horror movie on a show called "Screaming Yellow Theater." He worked at WFLD, channel 32, in Chicago, one of those low-budget UHF stations where it wasn't unusual for a picture to fall off the wall during a live production.

Anyhow, White Sox teammate Pat Kelly and I were asked to appear with Svengoolie for some kind of charity. We were just kids and when somebody from the publicity office said "show up and go on television" we didn't argue. We loved it. We even showed up for "Screaming Yellow Theater" in full White Sox uniform.

Svengoolie had this plan: He would hide in his fake coffin—dressed in cape and tails, of course—and then rise up at the opening of the telecast and squirt us with a water gun.

That didn't sound like much fun to me. So I improvised. As soon as Svengoolie settled into his coffin, I hustled up a hammer and nails. Wham-wham-wham. The coffin was nailed shut.

Now the show opens and I'm looking into the TV camera saying something like "Hi, I'm Jay Johnstone of the Chicago White Sox and this is my friend, Pat Kelly. That noise you hear (I think our Dracula look-alike was running out of air) is Svengoolie. He'll be with you shortly."

It just seemed like the thing to do.

I'm sure that's how relief pitcher Moe Drabowsky felt one night in Kansas City when he called the opposing dugout, imitated Alvin Dark's voice, and told Lew Krause to warm up.

First, though, let me tell you about the first time I met Moe. I was at one of Larry McTague's restaurants in New York City and Larry said, "Jay, I'd like you to meet Moe Drabowsky."

With that, Moe dropped his cocktail glass and reached out to shake my hand. I mean it shattered all over the floor and he didn't blink an eye. I knew right away that this was my kind of guy.

Moe was with the Baltimore Orioles back in 1966 when he made his bullpen phone call in Kansas City. He had just been traded from Kansas City (then the Athletics) and still remembered all the phone extensions within the ballpark. So one night in the Oriole bullpen he was bored and decided to call some of his old friends in the KC bullpen.

Except that when KC's bullpen coach, Bobby Hoffman,

picked up the phone, Moe got carried away. He started imitating KC manager Dark's voice.

"Get Krause (Lew) hot in a hurry!" yelled Drabowsky, then hung up.

Well, Jim Nash was sailing along with a two-hitter for Kansas City and there was no way Dark needed a relief pitcher. But sure enough, the bullpen reacted to Moe's call. Krause jumped up and started pumping warm-up throws.

The Oriole bullpen guys could see everything from across the field, of course, and they're laughing like hell. Then, after about five minutes, Moe picks up the phone again and yells, "OK, sit him down."

How a good Polish boy like Drabowsky could imitate the Southern Baptist twang of Alvin Dark is beyond me, but he got away with it. The newspapers picked up on the story and a few days later Moe got a letter from some kid in Keokuk, Iowa, who said: "Baseball needs more nuts like you."

Moe started having fun on the phone back in the early 1960s when he played for Charlie Finley's Athletics. Charlie, you see, has a distinctive voice and, inasmuch as Drabowsky was the player rep, he had plenty of opportunity to study it. He got it down pretty good, too—so good that during the off-season he'd call other players and imitate Finley.

Once, for example, he called Wayne Causey and said: "Waaaayne, this is Mr. Finley, and I want to know if you are going to sign that contract or not."

"But Mr. Finley," said Causey, "I can't sign for $13,500."

Moe pulled the same stunt with Rocky Colavito and others. That way he knew how much everybody else was being offered and it helped him with his own negotiations.

Once, too, with Baltimore, he called Brooks Robinson when he was a guest on a radio talk show and said: "Mr. Robinson, this is Charlie Finley of the Kansas City Athletics, and I just want you to know how happy I am that we have completed the trade deal. You are now a member of my baseball team."

There was no trade, of course, but for a few minutes Brooks was in total panic.

Actually, I've learned a lot from Drabowsky about doing business on ballpark telephones. It sure saves on the phone bills. Moe, you see, was a stock broker during the days he played. He got a lot of business done from the bullpen phone. He'd even call New York to get stock quotations. The calls, of course, would be charged to the ballpark switchboard.

Once in Milwaukee, when the Braves were still there, Moe was in the Cubs' bullpen and Glen Hobbie was Chicago's starting pitcher. The Braves had a real murderer's row in those days—Eddie Mathews, Hank Aaron, Joe Adcock, etc.—and poor Hobbie was getting killed. Finally, Cubs' manager Bob Scheffing picked up the phone to call the bullpen.

There was only one problem. Moe had the bullpen phone tied up. Scheffing kept getting the busy signal and the Braves kept hitting bullets off Hobbie. Finally, somebody looked down from the bullpen and saw all of these guys waving towels from the dugout steps. That's when Moe decided it was time to get off the phone.

My favorite Moe Drabowsky telephone story, though, was when he used the bullpen phone to call Hong Kong and order 25 Chinese carry-out dinners.

He wanted them delivered to Los Angeles, where the Orioles were scheduled to arrive that night. But there was no deal. Moe wanted fortune cookies within three hours and the Chinese couldn't deliver.

Moe was also known in Baltimore as the Snake Man.

Actually, he just put some finishing touches on one of Frank Robinson's favorite hobbies. F. Robby would carry a rubber snake around in an attaché case and use it to frighten the Latin players on the Orioles. Latins hate snakes. At least, Latin ball players do. Robinson would throw his rubber snake into the back of a team bus and cause a riot.

Moe went just a tiny step further. He started using live snakes. I won't bore you with all of his snake stories, but suffice it to say he earned his nickname—so much so that when he was invited back to Baltimore in 1984 for a sports banquet, he felt compelled, at age 48, to offer an encore performance.

Moe showed up at the speakers' table with a brown paper sack, but anyone looking inside would only see toothpaste, shaving cream, and other toilet articles. They would not have seen the four-foot Florida King snake which was resting comfortably.

Once lunch started, Moe asked somebody to pass the rolls. Then, between his legs under the table, Moe removed all the rolls and put the King snake into the basket, under the folded napkin.

The next guy to ask for rolls was Brooks Robinson. What he got was this little black head peeking out at him, the tongue flicking out about a thousand times per second. That Brooks is still living is testimony to his strong heart.

I don't know whether Frank Robinson was ever annoyed that Drabowsky took over his snake routine, but my personal opinion is that great ideas are meant to be swiped. That's one thing I want to make clear. It doesn't bother me to use other people's brilliant schemes.

Rick Monday, former teammate and now an announcer with the Dodgers, keeps calling me a "plagiarist," but I'm not sure I know what that means and I'm positive he doesn't.

He's probably referring to the time I asked for just a little help in compiling my Jay Johnstone All-Crazy Team.

A group of Dodgers—Jerry Grote, Jerry Reuss, and

Monday—were sitting at the end of the dugout in Houston back in 1981 and they noticed me, down at the other end, writing something on a piece of paper.

Finally, about the fourth or fifth inning, I went down to them and said "Hey, I need some help with my All-Crazy Team. Think of some names for me and what position they play . . . coaches, managers, everything."

So we sat there and threw out names—one guy would mention one name, somebody else another, until I finally got an entire team picked, substitutes and everything.

It wasn't a bad way to pass the time during a boring game. But then we flew back to Los Angeles and one of the guys bought a newspaper at the airport. And there, spread across the sports page, was "Jay Johnstone's All-Crazy Team."

"Hey, Jay," Monday asked, "how come you get the credit and none of your committee members even got mentioned?"

"This was my list, guys," I said, "I don't need any of your help. Besides, who got the headlines?"

But the next day there was another article quoting Billy Martin of the Yankees, ripping into me for listing some of Martin's ex-Yankee teammates.

"Where does a crazy flake like Jay Johnstone get off calling somebody else a flake?" Martin had said.

I go back into the clubhouse and say "Hey, you guys really got me into trouble. I'm telling everyone this was a committee thing."

"Right," says Monday. "You wanted headlines, you got 'em."

But I look at it this way: the seeds of laughter have always been in baseball; certain guys just enjoy making them grow.

Jerry Reuss and I, for example, certainly weren't the first ball players to dress like groundskeepers and drag the infield.

Jim Colborn, now a pitching coach for the Iowa (AAA) Cubs, did it back in 1974 when he was a pitcher for the Milwaukee Brewers (after playing under Leo Durocher with the Cubs, Jimmy probably needed a few laughs).

He even had to do his act bare-legged. County Stadium groundskeepers in those days wore lederhosen, the leather short pants with straps, so Colborn borrowed a pair and ran out to clean up around first base. But they didn't have big-screen scoreboard-vision in those days and a lot of fans didn't realize what was happening.

Jim always tried to do something unusual on the final day of the season—something to send him into the off-season with a smile. Once in Milwaukee he showed up at home plate on closing day dressed as an umpire. He took out the chest protector and game balls (real ump Bill Deegan had given him permission) and met with the managers, Ralph Houk of Detroit and his own boss, Alex Grammas.

Grammas didn't even recognize Colborn until Houk said, "Have a nice winter, Alex," and Jimmy followed with "Have a nice winter, Alex." Then Grammas recognized the voice, saw one of his pitchers wearing the umpire's uniform, and almost fainted.

And as soon as Alex said a word, Colborn gave him a mock ejection. All of Jim's teammates, meanwhile, were trying to get him to kick them out so they could go home early.

Ken McMullen (also a former major leaguer) and Colborn have been trying to purchase a minor league baseball franchise. One of these days they'll make it official and I'll guarantee you one thing: when you go to their games, you will be allowed to laugh.

I've always been intrigued, actually, by the way "ball-park humor" is passed from one era of ball players to another. Remember, for example, our Green Hornet pranks from Dodgertown?

When Jim Lefebvre was in spring training with the Dodgers, at least ten years earlier, he was the Green Phantom. We just kept the color and changed the name of the mysterious practical joker of Indian River County.

Actually, Tom Lasorda was very much involved in the origin of the Phantom. He was the Dodgers' Triple A manager then and one of Lefebvre's closest buddies. They spent many hours together—working out, going to dinner, just walking at night and talking baseball, whatever. That they later got into a fight and still haven't patched up their differences has probably bothered both of them. But that's baseball and that's life, I guess.

Anyhow, here's how the Green Phantom was born. One night Lefebvre went to pick up Lasorda for dinner and found him in the whirlpool. Tom didn't want anyone to know, however, because he loved to ride people about being in the training room. "You can't make the club in a tub," he used to say.

Well, the next morning Jim slipped into the training room and placed this sign "U.S.S. Lasorda," on the whirlpool. Then he got a bottle of that green mouthwash, Scope, which in those days called itself "Green Phantom" in an advertising campaign, and put it in Lasorda's locker with a note saying, "Once a day will help you—the Green Phantom."

From there the pranks grew. Jim got some Black Flag roach killer and labeled it "Tom Lasorda Spray Deodorant" and put it into his locker. Lasorda got so mad that he called aside Wes Parker and—of all people—Lefebvre, and assigned them to "find out who this Green Phantom guy is."

Then Joe Moeller and Lefebvre took all of Lasorda's clothes out of his locker and dyed them green. I mean everything. Shoes, bat, uniform, everything. By the end of spring, apparently everybody on that Dodger club was involved, at one time or another, in a Green Phantom prank.

And Don Sutton, who's quite a poet, would compose an appropriate note to go with every prank. The Phantom always left one of Sutton's calling cards.

Once they raided Lasorda's locker and staged it so he could catch some of the guys in the act but would find this note: "You only caught some of the Phantom's helpers. I will strike once more tonight." In the meantime, Lefebvre had slipped into Lasorda's room to short-sheet the bed.

Once after the Dodgertown St. Patrick's Day party, Lasorda returned to his room about 2:30 A.M. to find it totally empty. Everything was gone—bed, curtains, rug, dresser, everything but a little green ball and a note from Sutton which read: "If you want your stuff, look in Claude Osteen's shoe."

Now Lasorda wakes up clubhouse man Nobe Kawano at 3 A.M. and they go into the locker room to look into Osteen's shoe. There was another note which said "look in Jim Brewer's jock," and they kept going from clue to clue like kids on a scavenger hunt. Finally, they found the final note which told Lasorda to add up all of the uniform numbers and it would tell him where to find his stuff. It was the room next to his own.

A good one, too, was when Lefebvre got owner Walter O'Malley's permission to take the tires off his golf cart, which was as sacred to him as a golden chariot. They hid the tires under Lasorda's bed. Then O'Malley woke him up and asked him if he knew anything about the missing tires. "I don't know what you're talking about," said Lasorda, but just then O'Malley pulled the tires out from under his bed.

The whole spring went like that. Once they filled Lasorda's room—and I mean filled it to the ceiling—with balled-up newspapers. It was like a room filled with foam.

And, finally, on the last day of spring training, they announced they would reveal the true identity of the Green Phantom. Everybody was gathered around the swimming pool for a barbeque and Lefebvre showed up with this green outfit and white mask.

"Here he is," somebody announced, and Lasorda snatched the mask off. But there was another mask underneath, then a stocking mask under that. And each time Lasorda would grab at something, the Pranksters would all edge closer to the pool. But Lasorda didn't realize what was happening.

Finally, Lefebvre revealed his face and Lasorda screamed "You!"

"Yes," Jim said, "and for my final act as the Green Phantom. . . ."

Lasorda went right into the pool.

Lefebvre lists those memories as unforgettable, but says that it still bothers him that he and Lasorda later became enemies.

I don't know how it happened. Maybe Lasorda felt Lefebvre was trying to undermine him when he coached with the Dodgers. Whatever happened is between them, but they've both been very close to me. Lasorda has always been one of my biggest boosters and I can never forget those early morning hours Lefebvre and I spent together with his father, hitting tennis balls off those batting tees.

Let's face it. Much of baseball's hierarchy is built on past relationships. People play together and coach together for decades. They can't help forming strong relationships, whether as friends or enemies.

Chuck Tanner and I, for example, go back almost 20 years in organized baseball. We sure had our differences early but Tanner now claims he helped "tame" me, and he probably did.

I do remember the day he tried to test me with a fungo

bat. Actually, he tried to run my butt into the ground. It must have been 1966 or 1967, back when Tanner was the Double A coach in the California Angels' system, and he decided to keep me after practice one day for a little one-on-one fly ball practice.

He had the fungo bat. I had the glove and young legs.

He ran me left, he ran me right. He ran me forward and back. But I never said a word. I just ran, caught the baseballs, and threw them back.

Finally, when we were finished. I asked Chuck to come over and meet this gorgeous blonde who was sitting by herself in the grandstand. He hadn't even noticed her. It was my wife-to-be, Mary Jayne, who had driven down from Los Angeles to visit me.

But I had a problem. She had her car and I had my new Thunderbird. I loved the T-Bird but preferred to ride back to the hotel with Mary Jayne.

"Would you drive my car back?" I asked Tanner. I could tell he'd never driven a car as sporty as a T-bird before, but he wouldn't admit it. Besides, how could he turn me down after trying to run me into the ground?

Finally, he figured out how to drive the car and off we went.

Tanner later told me that he became convinced, on that day when I didn't complain, that someday I would become a big leaguer. He also reminded me this spring that I had lasted in the major leagues longer than any player he had ever managed. Those are meaningful words from a guy like Tanner.

Another former teammate and current friend, Don Stanhouse, visited the Dodgers when they played this season in Houston (he's in the oil and real estate business in Dallas) and reminded me of the gig I most hated missing.

It was the hospital visit paid by Stanhouse and Reuss to Reggie Smith in a Los Angeles hospital. I had a speaking engagement that night and couldn't go along.

Reggie had undergone shoulder surgery and one Sunday evening, after a day game, Reuss and Stanhouse headed for the hospital, loaded down with fried chicken and Scotch whiskey. Then they recruited some nurses to dress them in white jackets.

"Do you have any with blood on them?" asked Reuss, but they didn't. They didn't have any surgical masks, either, but they taped easy-wipe towels over their faces and headed for Reggie's room.

"Get 'em out of here!" Reggie yelled to the nurse, but it was too late. He was in for a party.

Little did Reuss and Stanhouse know they'd put too much Scotch in Reggie, messed up his sugar content, and forced them to keep him in the hospital a day longer. But it was worth it.

It was good running with Stan the Man Unusual because in addition to being a free spirit, he was a "gamer." I always looked at myself the same way. Sure, we played hard, but nobody worked harder either.

A vivid memory of "House": Finally, I had gotten a chance to start and had struck out four times. And I refused to go home until I worked out the problem. It was about 10 P.M. after a day game and I was down there in the hitting cage. My hands were raw. I had found a flaw in my swing and I made Stanhouse stay there, acting as a sounding board, until I got it corrected. He was there in his underwear and I had bleeding hands five hours after the game was over. I've never forgotten that incident.

Hell, we did so many things together I know he can't remember all of them. Once on St. Patrick's Day we painted Tom Lasorda's refrigerator green and painted Steve Garvey's bats the same color.

Stanhouse, you see, always shared my feelings about taking baseball too seriously. You just can't do it and survive. The game itself is easy enough to play and if you have talent, you can be among the best.

But it is a little boys' game and if you can't have a good time while making a living, why do it? I don't remember playing baseball as a kid all those years and not having a good time. People put pressure on ball players by saying "you gotta do this, or you gotta do that, because you make so much money," but it doesn't hold water unless you can also enjoy yourself.

Stanhouse and I had a serious talk, if you can believe it, this spring in Houston. He told me what it had been like for him since leaving baseball. Sure, he's got money—lots of it, thanks to the multi-year, guaranteed contract he had when the Dodgers released him.

"But give the kids a message for me," said Stanhouse. "Tell them to bust their asses and stay in the game as long as they can . . . because it's a real world out there and that Disneyland ride they're on is going to end some day. I never thought it would, but it did."

Stan the Man Unusual also gave me some advice about this book. He told me to leave fifteen or twenty pages blank at the end, just to make readers wonder if we had forgotten anything. "Better yet," said Stanhouse, "leave the last twenty pages blank with a note which reads: 'If you can understand these next twenty pages, you probably know Jay Johnstone personally.' "

What a buddy.

Another buddy has been Steve (Boomer) Yeager, Dodger catcher and a walking hardware store. He's got a couple of screws holding one knee together and once had a broken bat stuck in his neck, but ol' Yang keeps hangin' in there and throwing out base runners. Yeager and I roomed together a couple of years at Dodgertown. Once we got involved in a head-on car wreck (no injuries, just a lot of explanations) on the first day of spring training. And I couldn't have roped Lasorda into his room without Yang's help.

Boomer has also been the team's sex symbol for years.

Don't ask me why. Females see Yeager's picture in the program (once they even saw it in *Playgirl* magazine) and start purring.

It's a good thing they can't hear him sing. When Boomer performed with Monday, Reuss, and me with the "Big Blue Wrecking Crew" after the 1981 World Series, he was by far the best singer. Of course that was after they added an echo chamber and backup singers to drown him out.

The rest of us, of course, were perfect.

Whether or not Yang can sing was not the issue there, however. The issue is that a bunch of guys on a championship team got an idea and decided to have some fun with it. Championship teams always seem to have that one thing in common: togetherness. True, it doesn't always stay that long and it's sometimes difficult for outsiders to recognize (those Oakland A's teams of the early 1970s fought each other almost as much as they fought other teams), but it's always there.

Yet, does the winning bring togetherness or does togetherness cause the winning? I think the answer is a combination of both.

Mike Shannon, frequent visitor at Charlie Gitto's restaurant in St. Louis and broadcast partner of Cardinals announcer Jack Buck, tells a unique story about the 1968 world championship Cardinals.

They had clinched the National League pennant (there were no divisional playoffs then) in Houston and everybody celebrated on the chartered flight into San Francisco. Then they decided to keep the party going. Most of the players congregated on California Street and, even though they had a game to play the next night, the whooping and drinking continued.

But, inasmuch as San Francisco saloons are public, it wasn't exactly a private party. A lot of other patrons also joined in the festivities and, as happens, a reporter observed the Cardinals at their cork-popping best.

Headlines the next day read: "Wine, Women, and Song"

and described the Cardinals in such bad condition that the writer boldly predicted: "Gaylord Perry will probably throw a no-hitter against them."

And he was right. That's exactly what happened. Perry mowed down the hungover Cardinals. But guess what? Once the Cards sobered up they got mad. And one night later, Ray Washburn threw a no-hitter against the Giants. It's the only time in history that teams traded back-to-back no-hitters.

Shannon's favorite story: he was playing third base against the Phillies, managed in those days by Gene Mauch. Shannon didn't like Mauch. He felt Mauch had shown him up when he first came into the big leagues.

On this day, Mauch inserted pitcher Grant Jackson as a pinch-runner against the Cardinals and Jackson advanced, sliding, from first to third on a base hit.

But as he stood to dust himself off Shannon said, ever so politely. "Excuse me, but would you step aside for a moment while I kick this bag back into position."

Jackson obliged.

Then, standing between Jackson and the bag, arms hanging at his side, Shannon said, "Uuuuuuh, Mr. Jackson."

Jackson then saw Shannon casually holding the baseball in his bare hand.

"Oh, shit," said Jackson. "Mauch will kill me."

"Sorry," said Shannon, in no hurry to apply the final touch.

"Mike," pleaded Jackson, "isn't there anything we can do about this? A free dinner? You need a wristwatch? Anything?"

"Sorry," said Shannon. "I've already showed the ball to the ump."

"But I'm telling you, Mauch will kill me."

"Don't take it personally," said Shannon. "This one is for Mauch, anyhow."

With that, he tagged Jackson and the inning was over.

But back to team togetherness. Every team has its own traditions, its own superstitions. Maybe there's a certain ritual someone remembers that gets the team charged up. But there's one tradition shared by every team in the National League.

At the corner of Belmont Avenue and Sheridan Road in Chicago stands a statue of General Phillip Sheridan, hero of the Civil War. The Gutzon Borglum sculpture, erected on July 17, 1924, depicts General Sheridan, mounted on a rearing horse, in combat.

Riding high above the busy intersection and an island of grass (a dog walker's haven), General Sheridan is ostensibly rallying his troops during the battle of Shenandoah Valley, 1864.

"Back to the front, boys!" is what the Civil War hero is supposed to be shouting, and any patriot, using just a little imagination, can surely gaze upon this replica and sense the sounds and smells of battle.

And, from the proper angle, he can also see the horse's testicles.

They are the "Horse's Balls of Chicago," and they've become part of baseball tradition.

Every National League team, you see, when visiting Chicago to play the Cubs, travels from the hotel to Wrigley Field by bus. And every bus driver takes the same route— north on Outer Lake Shore Drive, exit at Belmont, right turn at Belmont and Sheridan on the Inner Drive, then north to Addison Street.

Every team bus passes the statue of General Sheridan.

Every busload of ball players peeks at the horse's balls.

Except for those who refuse to look. Different players have different attitudes about the horse's balls. It's a matter of superstition.

If a player is in a slump, for example, a teammate might say, "Look at the horse's balls and it'll change your luck."

Or if a player is going well, somebody from the back of the bus might yell, "Don't look at the horse's balls . . . it'll bring you bad luck."

And as players have changed from team to team, veterans have indoctrinated rookies or newcomers from the American League. Peek or no peek, nobody really ignores the horse's balls. At last look (May 1985), they were reddish-orange, compliments of the San Francisco Giants, traditionalists and patriots all.

Pitcher Mike Krukow didn't apply the painter's brush, but he was the master planner and schemer.

Actually, he started during the 1984 season. Sitting in the Giants' bus with Steve Nicosia—but just one seat behind rookies Frank Williams and Jeff Cornell—Krukow went into his routine.

"Tradition is dead in this league," said Krukow.

"What do you mean?" said one of the rookies.

"I'll tell you what I mean," said Krukow. "You guys see those horse's balls? I just can't believe that nobody has painted them. It has always been a tradition that when a team visits Chicago for the first time each year, the rookies on the team paint their team's colors on the horse's balls."

"But what if you get caught?" asked Williams.

"That's the best part," said Krukow. "Hell, when Bruce Sutter and I were rookies with the Cubs, we got crocked one day at the Cubby Bear Lounge and went over and painted those balls blue. We got caught, too, but it was great. They just take you down to the neighborhood precinct and make you sign your name in this book.

"It's like a *Who's Who* . . . names like Henry Aaron, Ernie Banks, Willie Mays . . . they were all rookies who painted the horse's balls. They all signed the book."

And just in case the hook wasn't firmly implanted, Krukow added: "But rookies nowadays don't have any heart. They're all pussies."

That did it. When the bus passed General Sheridan's statue the next day, the balls were painted orange. The Giants' rookies had struck at night.

And this year Krukow did it again. This time the painters were Williams (a genuine patriot) and rookie Robby Deer, a shy, polite young man who needed a lot of persuading.

But Krukow closed the deal by saying, "You can't deface the statue, you know, because it's a fact that when there is a statue of a horse with two legs off the ground, it means the rider was killed in action. If only one leg is raised, that means he was wounded.

"See that statue. One leg is raised. That means General Sheridan was wounded in battle. It means he was a gamer, Robby!"

By the time Krukow finished, rookie Deer was almost hoping he'd get caught, just so he could sign that non-existent precinct register.

"Robby didn't get caught," Krukow told me a few weeks later. "And the paint he used was more red than orange, but he did a helluva job. Guys on our bus went nuts the next day when we drove past and saw those brightly colored balls.

"In fact, it really rallied the troops."

Isn't that what General Sheridan had in mind?

"

Best Towns in Which to Get into Trouble: New York, Chicago, San Francisco, Montreal, and Atlanta.

"

CHAPTER

10

JAY JOHNSTONE'S ALL-CRAZY TEAM AND LIST OF BESTS

"The most amazing thing I've ever seen at Dodger Stadium was Jay Johnstone, in uniform, in line for a hot dog at one of our concession stands after the game had already started."

Fred Claire
Vice President
Los Angeles Dodgers

One of my complaints about major league clubhouses is that the lockers aren't big enough to store all of my props.

That's probably what happened to my Star Patrol helmet. I probably left it out and somebody couldn't resist it. But at least I saved the victory glasses, umbrella hats, and PRC microphone.

Lou Brock gave me a supply of the Brock-a-brella hats. All kinds, different colors. They're great for sticking your head out of the dugout during a rain delay. Cameramen never miss you.

The PRC microphone never makes the papers, but it's caused grief to more than a few film and videotape editors. Just when they think they've got their own mike identity in front of the camera—you've seen all those ABC and NBC ititials on the ends of mikes—I attach the PRC mike, which is actually a fake, rubberized penis head—to the end of a bat and thrust it into the middle of the interview. It takes a steady person to keep from breaking up when he sees that PRC Network has arrived.

Somebody sent me the victory glasses. They're just oversized, gag sunglasses that I put on when victory is in sight, just like Red Auerbach lighting up his cigar.

Can you believe Joe Garagiola criticized me for wearing them in the Dodgers dugout? Here we were in the World Series, and Joe-the-serious-broadcaster is making some comment about my glasses not being proper. I suppose Joe never did anything crazy when he played. He was only the original Bob Uecker.

Or perhaps Joe just hasn't forgotten about the time he was interviewing Richie Allen and I dropped a firecracker between his feet. He did lose his train of thought after Allen jumped into his arms.

And because of his crack about my victory glasses, Garagiola has been disqualified from consideration for my All-Crazy Team. It's just as well. He'd never beat out Harry Caray. Anybody who sings "Take Me Out to the Ball Game" as badly and as often as Caray has to be nuts. I love him, but he's the craziest.

JAY JOHNSTONE'S ALL-CRAZY TEAM

Manager: Leo Durocher
Coaches: Hank Bauer, Art Fowler, Larry Sherry
Starting pitchers: Bo Belinsky, Steve Carlton, Sam Mc-Dowell, Jim Rooker, Stan Williams, Bert Blyleven, Jerry Reuss, Bill Lee
Long relief: Greg Minton, Bill Caudill
Short relief: Don Stanhouse, Moe Drabowsky, Tug McGraw, Sparky Lyle

First base: Joe Pepitone, Norm Cash
Second base: Rich Hebner, Phil Garner
Third base: Doug Rader, Al Gallagher
Shortstop: Jim Fregosi, Kurt Bevacqau
Outfield: Jim Piersall, Lou Piniella, Curt Blefary, Jay Johnstone
Utility players: Danny Walton, Mike Shannon, Bob Allison
Trainer: Charlie Saad
Disabled list: Randy Jones, George Brunet, Mike Kekich, Jerry Johnson, Bob Reynolds, Charlie Sands
Announcer: Harry Caray
Honorable mention: Mickey Mantle, Boog Powell, Dean Chance, Don Drysdale, Johnny Podres, Dick Schofield, Lew Burdette, Dick Green, Bob Lee, Lee Thomas, Dick Stuart, Rick Dempsey, Joe Torre, and John Lowenstein.

JAY JOHNSTONE'S LIST OF BESTS

Airline food: Ozark
Prettiest stewardesses: PSA
Best spring training cities: Phillies in Clearwater, White Sox in Sarasota, Angels in Palm Springs, Giants in Scottsdale, Yankees in Fort Lauderdale
Best spring facilities: Dodgertown, Vero Beach
Worst spring sites: Tucson, Yuma, Winter Haven
Best shopping towns for wives: New York, Dallas, Chicago, Montreal, San Francisco, Atlanta
Best hitting coach: Billy DeMars
Best baseball writer: Bill Conlin, *Philadelphia Daily News*
Worst writer: Any and all looking for sensationalism, dissension
Best fungo hitter: Jimmy Reese
Best uniforms: Astros, Phillies, Dodgers, Yankees, Angels
Best towns for suntan: Houston, San Diego, Cincinnati, St. Louis, Atlanta

Best announcers: Vin Scully, (Dodgers), Harry Caray (Cubs), Jerry Coleman (Padres), Marty Brenaman (Reds), Harry Kalas (Phillies)

Most knowledgeable fans: Yankees, Cubs, Phillies, Mets, Red Sox

Best mascot: San Diego Chicken, Phillie Fanatic

Best towns in which to play: New York, Chicago, Los Angeles, San Diego, Atlanta

Best road clubhouses: Cincinnati, Atlanta, Montreal, St. Louis, San Diego, Philadelphia

Best, wildest cab ride cities: New York, San Francisco, Chicago, Montreal, Philadelphia

Best parks for hitting: Philadelphia, Chicago (Wrigley), St. Louis, Atlanta, Cincinnati

Best hotels: Houston Shamrock Hilton, San Diego Sheraton, Montreal Sheraton, San Francisco Hilton, New York Grand, Atlanta Hilton

Best clubhouse pioneer: Joe Pepitone (first to use hair dryer)

Best bus rides to ballpark: New York, Philadelphia, Los Angeles, San Francisco, Montreal

Best subways: Montreal

Most harrowing train rides: New York

Shortest subway ride: Philadelphia

Slowest: San Francisco cable cars

Oldest: Chicago elevated trains

Tightest uniforms: Phillies

Best restaurant towns: Chicago, New York, San Francisco, Montreal, Los Angeles

Best clubhouse spread: San Francisco, Cincinnati, St. Louis, New York, Atlanta

Best towns in which to get into trouble: New York, Chicago, San Francisco, Montreal, Atlanta

Best fan wave: New York

Worst fan wave: Montreal

Best ballpark entertainment: Los Angeles, Philadelphia, New York (Yankees)

Best traveling secretaries: Tommy Ferguson of Angels (retired), Billy DeLury of Dodgers, John "Doc" Mattei of Padres, Eddie Ferenz of Phillies

Best underground tapes: Lee Elia of Cubs, Lasorda tape on Dave Kingman

"

Mark Fidrych talked to baseballs. Don Stan-house shared his post-game beer with stuffed monkeys and stuffed frogs. Mickey Hatcher put a pig in Lasorda's office. And Pat Putnam had a Shamu the Whale routine: he'd coil inside the whirlpool, spring out, and snatch hot dogs with his teeth.

And *I'm* nuts?

CHAPTER

11

IF YOU THINK
I'M NUTS...

"I'm just glad Jay could finish this book before the men in white coats came to take him away."

Ron Cey

Danny Ozark once said: "The unusual thing about Johnstone is that he thinks he's normal and everyone else is nuts."

I don't see anything unusual about that at all.

Tom Lasorda once fixed up Ernie Broglio on a date with a female impersonator.

Leo Durocher once offered Joe Pepitone $50 to dump a salad on a sportswriter's lap. Pepi called his bluff by countering with a $100 offer.

Rocky Bridges once said about playing exhibition games against teams from Japan: "I enjoy playing them, but two hours later I want to play them again."

Dodgers announcer Jerry Doggett once said, "Well, the weatherman said 50 percent chance of rain and he might be right."

Paul Owens once went to a civic luncheon without his glasses and handed an announcement to a blind man to read.

And I'm nuts?

John Lowenstein likes to attack cakes with a bat. Bill Caudill once kept a deerstalker hat and cape, calabash pipe, magnifying glass, handcuffs, and two stuffed pink panthers in his locker.

Lee Elia said about Caudill: "He's not a high-ball pitcher. He's a highball drinker."

Umpire Bruce Froemming once kicked an entire press box out of a game. Dean Chance would hide his spitball by turning away from homeplate, cupping his hands, and spitting on the ball.

Mark Fidrych talked to baseballs. Don Stanhouse shared his post-game beer with stuffed monkeys and stuffed frogs. Bill Lee got fined $250 for sprinkling marijuana on his pancakes.

Mickey Hatcher put a pig in Lasorda's office. Pat Putnam had a "Shamu the Whale" routine. He would coil inside the whirlpool, spring out, and snatch hotdogs with his teeth.

Bert Blyleven gave chewing tobacco to his Little League players. Richie Zisk filled Rene Lachemann's hotel bed with Jello. Doug Rader liked to hide among clubhouse ceiling pipes and spit tobacco juice on victims below.

And they're calling me a Moon Man?

Al Hrabosky carried voodoo pins and dolls and once bit off the head of a fan's parrot. Joe Charboneau removed a tattoo with a razor blade, and Ross Grimsley once snapped a losing streak by consulting a witch. Dave Goltz put a fish in Tom Lasorda's toilet bowl.

Rick Reichardt stole razor blades from the clubhouse, forgot he had them, then sliced his own hand when he reached into his pocket. Bill Melton, wearing no shoes, stole a motorcycle in Chicago. And when Reichardt blew a fly ball, he blamed it on winds that were "diametrically opposed."

Jim Kern used a different hotfoot technique from mine. He would dip cotton balls in rubbing alcohol, then light the match. Instant screams.

Dave Heaverlo's wife made him grow hair back on his shaved head because he was scaring their kid. Rick Bosetti says he's on a mission to urinate on every major league field. That's why he favors interleague play. Says Rick: "To water that grass in beautiful Wrigley Field would be a dream come true."

Dan Quisenberry tried to shove a shower nozzle down his throat after giving up a home run. Mark Lemongello once bit his own shoulder. Steve Howe cut holes in the leotard crotches of Ram football players before a charity skit.

Rader once suggested on a TV show that if Little Leaguers wanted to grow up big and strong they should eat Willie McCovey bubblegum cards.

Dizzy Dean once built a bonfire in front of the St. Louis dugout. Another time he placed a cake of ice on home plate to "cool off my fast ball." Ted Kluzewski put a snake in Monk Meyer's back pocket.

Moe Drabowsky once got on the dugout phone, imitated Alvin Dark's voice, and ordered a pitcher to warm up. He also used that phone for international phone calls. Billy Loes once refused to pitch unless Buzzy Bavasi would buy him a new boxer dog.

Tug McGraw, when asked if he preferred grass to artificial turf, replied, "I never smoked turf."

Gorman Thomas put a squid into a teammate's glove. Joaquin Andujar has been known to shower wearing his uniform. Mike Norris said he was so bummed out during the 1981 strike that he checked into a hotel just so he could imagine he was on a road trip. Tim Stoddard wanted to tattoo a manager's uniform into a concrete wall with a jack gun.

And it was Steve McCatty, after hearing about Charlie Finley's heart surgery, who said, "It took eight hours . . . seven and a half to find the heart."

Flake? Who's a flake? Have you ever heard of Jackie Brandt? He gets credit for the term. When he was a rookie outfielder for the St. Louis Browns in 1956, a teammate noticed that "things seem to flake off his mind and disappear." Jackie once played 27 holes of golf in 101-degree heat before a doubleheader. So what's strange about that? Caudill once handcuffed Mike Moore to a bullpen railing and left him.

Baseball writer Randy Youngman once asked Bill Lee to describe the meaning of life. "The meaning of life. . . . " said Lee, pausing, "You can find it on Fernwood Court in Topanga Canyon."

"Where's that?"

"It's where the dragon lives."

I rest my case, Danny Ozark.

I even came to the conclusion during the spring of 1985 that I was more normal than many of the baseball writers of today. You think ball players are nomads? Try keeping track of one of those guys. At least the clubhouse is my home on the road. Those guys live with only two burning concerns: Can I make deadline, and what time does the bar close? Their official stationery is a cocktail napkin. Take away their computer terminals and disconnect the telephones, and they couldn't function.

Actually, I like sportswriters. Announcers, too. That, in itself, makes me different from most ball players of this era. But I've learned to understand their priorities and realize that most of them have a code of ethics that can be understood. As always happens, the irresponsible actions of a few often give the group a bad name.

I must say, though, that the group covering the Dodgers in Vero Beach last spring was unique. Consider some of their names: Chopper, Pig, Mouse, The Assassin, and One-a-Day. There was a radio man down the hall named the

Steamer, and somebody was asking whatever happened to Rat, Pox, Teddy Bear, Cyclops, Hamster, Werewolf Mort, Indian, and The Schmuck?

What was this, a press room or a menagerie? Can you imagine being a vice president of the Dodgers and walking into the press room to introduce the new commissioner, Peter Ueberroth?

"Commissioner, I'd like you to meet the Dodgers writers, Chopper and Pig, this is the commissioner, Mouse, One-a-Day, Mr. Ueberroth. And over here . . . The Assassin."

Don't ask me why Los Angeles writers don't have real names. Maybe they all came from Disney Studios. They privately refer to ball players, incidentally, as "oafs." But it's an affectionate term—isn't it?

Teddy Bear is John Strege of *The Register* (Orange County), predecessor to One-a-Day on the Dodger beat. The Bear earned considerable respect from his peers when, after having several cocktails on a chartered team flight, he prohibited Lasorda from sitting next to him by saying, "You're invading my privacy."

Mouse (Ken Gurnick, *Herald-Examiner*) got his nickname because of his size. He's about five feet tall. The boys tried to fix him up once with a midget waitress, but he rebelled when she started calling him Kareem.

Chopper is Bob Hunter of the *Daily News*. He has covered the Dodgers since their arrival in Los Angeles and has been a sportswriter for 50 years. He celebrated this spring by drinking two diet Cokes in the same evening.

Why the name Chopper? The late Dodger owner, Walter O'Malley, loved to play poker in the Dodgertown press room. So did Hunter. And whenever there was a high-low pot to be divided, Walter would always bellow, "Chop it up," to Hunter, who would divide the money.

Chopper has traveled so much in baseball that he once called home, awakened his wife at 8:00 A.M., and heard her say, "Bob who?"

On another occasion, she took him to the airport for a

road trip and said, "Have fun . . . and stay out of trouble."

Replied Chopper: "Make up your mind, woman."

One-a-Day (Randy Youngman, of *The Register*) got his unusual name by being a pitcher in college. He wore Coke bottles for glasses and plunked an average of one hitter every game.

The Pig is Gordon Verrell of the *Long Beach Press-Telegram*. I think his nickname came from the paper mess he creates every spring in the corner of the press room.

Verrell once lost a car on a Florida beach. He reportedly drove over there ("to see if the box scores would float"), got stuck, and hitchhiked back to Dodgertown. The following spring he wrote a strong letter to Dodgers officials, suggesting he be provided a vehicle with four-wheel drive.

The Assassin, a.k.a. Terry Johnson of the *Daily Breeze*, earned a place in my Hall of Fame by once eating an Atlanta bar tab worth $85. He felt he and his pals were being overcharged, so he simply gulped down the check, burped, giggled, and departed. Why nicknamed The Assassin? Because when Tiny Tim showed up one night and sang "God Bless America" at Gilley's in Pasadena, Texas, T.J. wanted to kill him.

Gordon Edes of the *Times* and Matt McHale of the *Pasadena Star-News* are also beat regulars with the Dodgers, but they're so weird they don't even have nicknames. John Lowe was a Dodgers regular, but after being forced to sleep in a Dodgertown closet one spring (his roomie snored), John decided to move to Philadelphia.

For the past three years, Dodgers writers have had their fun with Lasorda. I'm not talking about real stories after real games. Writers and managers will always have differences in that arena. I'm talking about fun away from either job.

Like on the Wrigley Field scoreboard.

Lasorda, you see, has a cadre of followers. Bo-bos. Maybe that name comes from Little Bo Peep and all those sheep who followed her around. Whatever, Tommy has a lot of them—usually relatives, salesmen, or somebody who has something to do with free food.

And each year when the Dodgers visit Chicago, the Bo-bo pass list seems to grow. It has become so large, in fact, that when Tommy's followers are all seated behind home-plate it becomes Bo-bo Row.

Mouse, irritated one year because he couldn't squeeze past the Bo-bos to get into Lasorda's office after a game, declared a miniwar. He took a press box collection. He then bribed the Cubs' scoreboard operator and public address announcer. And in the third inning, players in the dugout and fans throughout the park heard: "Wrigley Field extends a special welcome from restaurants all over America, Tommy's Bo-bos!" At the same time, "Tommy's Bo-bos" flashed across the scoreboard message board.

It didn't match dragging the infield or tying Lasorda into his room, but for sportswriters it wasn't bad.

An unidentified LA sportswriter pulled another fast one last summer in San Francisco during All-Star Game festivities.

Actually, it was a case of mistaken identity. The writer, wearing a three-piece suit and sipping vodka, was approached during a cocktail party by another writer (non-sports) of the *San Francisco Examiner*.

"Are you an owner?" asked the San Franciscan.

"No," said the LA writer, pausing, "But I once was."

"Oh, really? Who are you?"

"I'm Bill Wrigley. I used to own the Cubs."

"Well, how do you find San Francisco hospitality?"

"This is great. I didn't know how much J missed it."

End of conversation. Except that two hours later, after the LA writer had consumed several more vodkas from Russia, he was approached again by the same man, now carrying a small notebook.

"Are you enjoying the party, Mr. Wrigley?"

"Oh, yes. I've seen a lot of old friends."

"Would you ever think of getting back into baseball?"

"Well, actually, I've already had conversations with Bob Lurie about buying the San Francisco Giants."

The *Examiner* reporter began scribbling furiously.

"And I'll tell you one thing," said the LA visitor, warming to his role. "If I do buy the Giants, I'll tear down Candlestick Park and build a new stadium downtown."

The story made page one headlines the next day in the *San Francisco Examiner*. Associated Press picked up the story, complete with erroneous quotes. Then both Chicago newspapers, *Tribune* and *Sun-Times*, ran the story. Wrigley's picture even got into print, along with angry denials.

"I wasn't even in San Francisco," said Wrigley.

"Of course he wasn't," the LA writer told friends. "He didn't even go to Wrigley Field when he owned the Cubs."

Reporting sounds like a tough business to me. I'm glad I know how to drag infields.

There are times, however, when even the best practical joke cannot save a situation. There are times when a ball player must crawl within himself.

Or, like Tug McGraw, crawl himself into jail.

Some background: Tug and I were with the Phillies, and we were playing our rivals—our hated rivals—the Pirates, a doubleheader in Pittsburgh.

Things did not go so well. Not only did the Phils lose both games, there was a free-for-all brawl and our star thirdbaseman, Mike Schmidt, broke his thumb.

Things didn't improve after the game. Some big college kid was standing outside our bus screaming obscenities. I was standing with Danny Ozark in the doorway of the bus and asked him to stop. Instead, he got more abusive.

Now, I'm on the front step, and I reached out, grabbed him, and introduced his face to the side of the bus. We were all a little edgy. The guy must have been about 6'4" or 6'5", but by standing on the front step I was about even with him. He never knew what hit him and left him with a bloody nose.

As expected, though, he called the cops, and they came to our hotel looking for a "guy about 6'4" or 6'5"." I slipped out of our hotel and checked into another one. It was that kind of day.

About half the team, it seems, went out drinking that night. Bob Boone was still so mad that he ripped a big sign from behind the bar and started out the door with it. The bartender headed after him, but Richie Hebner, sitting on the last stool in the bar, stuck out one of his massive arms, lifted the guy up by the neck, and said, "That's my friend. If he wants that sign, he can have it."

Now the whole place is getting crazy, and McGraw is absolutely shit-faced drunk. Somehow, though, he knew what he had to do.

He took a taxi to the Pittsburgh police station, walked in, and said: "Hi, my name is Tug McGraw. I've had a tough day and night. I was losing pitcher in both games of a doubleheader, and I'm not responsible for what I do. Will you please put me into jail?"

"That's commendable, Mr. McGraw," said one of the desk cops, "but why don't you just go back to the hotel and sleep it off?"

"Dammit," screamed Tug, "I told you I'm not responsible. I want to go to jail."

"I'm sorry, Mr. McGraw, but we're not in the habit of locking up people just because they want to be locked up. Go back to the hotel and sleep it off."

"Listen, you fuckin' asshole. I want to go to fuckin' jail right now!"

"Lock him up," said the cop, who had heard enough.

He went in at 2:00 A.M., and the traveling secretary, Eddie Ferenz, got him out at 6:00 A.M.

But nobody else got hurt or into any fights. Drunk or not, I've got to figure ol' Tugger knew what he was doing.

Actually, there is very little to do in Pittsburgh at night except drink, win or lose.

I suspect, though, that the native Pittsburghers view visiting ball players as somewhat strange. I remember one night in 1979 when they did. It was during my half-season with the San Diego Padres, and I was out that night with Kurt Bevacqua and Randy Jones. And we were bored.

This was when that SWAT team show was big on television, however, so as we left the bar to head for the hotel, we decided to play SWAT. So picture this. Three grown men in suits and ties on the empty streets of Pittsburgh after midnight, making believe they're a SWAT team.

First we post guards around this building, then we're rushing around the corners, pretending we have rifles. Wherever the terrorists are, we go. Guys are rolling on the ground, leaping over fire hydrants, and barreling into the ivy. Jones landed on a sprinkler head, cut his pants, and bruised his knee. Bevacqua was crawling along the top of some wall. You'd have thought we were fourth-graders on the school playground.

Finally, somebody noticed this old drunk sitting on the sidewalk. He'd been there the whole time, just watching us and sipping out of his brown paper bag. The guy was grinning from ear to ear. He'd never had so much fun.

"Thought you were seeing things, didn't you, old-timer?" Randy said.

"What the hell," he said. "It's better than seeing elephants."

"

On this particular night, I was hitting seventh, and the first six batters got hits. But I never got to bat. Why? Because Marty Marion had a few drinks before coming to the park, and he kept waving the runners home. Three guys got thrown out at home, the last one by 20 feet. And I'm standing there with a bat in my hand, fresh out of high school, thinking, "This is professional baseball?"

"

CHAPTER

12

JUST GLAD
TO BE HERE

*"I'd like to see Jay play baseball forever because it
makes him a happy man. He's meant to play baseball.
A lot of them aren't."*

Mary Jayne Johnstone

It seems like only yesterday that a 19-year-old Angels
rookie named Jay Johnstone jumped back from home
plate in astonishment in Comiskey Park, Chicago.

I was astonished because the White Sox had one of those
automatic air jets that popped up from the middle of home
plate, went "whooosh," to clean away the dirt, then
disappeared.

Ex-teammate Tom Satriano reminded me that I had
immediately dropped my bat and started back toward the
dugout, proclaiming: "Whew . . . I knew this league was
fast, but I didn't even see that pitch!"

Even then, a smart-ass.

And it soon became evident that I was destined, no
matter what my desires, for a somewhat different kind of
career.

Fresh out of high school, 1963, I was assigned to San
Jose, the Angels' Single A affiliate, managed by ex-Cardinal
shortstop Marty Marion.

On this particular night, I was hitting seventh in the lineup, and the first six batters got base hits.

But I didn't get to bat. Why? Because Marion had a few drinks before coming to the ballpark that night and was managing from the third base coaching box.

He kept waving runners home. Three guys got thrown out at home plate, the last one by 20 feet. And I'm standing there with a bat in my hand—the seventh guy up after six hits, and there are three outs. I'm saying to myself, "This is professional baseball?"

I was always brash, I always had confidence. But I also worked hard. I wish those characteristics on every young man who comes into the major leagues today.

How brash? I remember once in Minnesota, while a young Angel, picking up the hotel telephone and calling Twins owner Calvin Griffith.

"Hi, my name is Jay Johnstone, and I'm in town with the Angels to play your team. But I'm having trouble with my batting stroke. Would you mind opening the park early so I could take some extra hitting?"

"I'll have to check with our grounds crew," said Griffith, after recovering from his surprise. "What was your name again? Johnstone? I'll get back to you."

When he called back, though, I wasn't available, and he talked with manager Lefty Phillips, instead. Phillips was appalled that one of his kids had called a major league owner. He apologized to Griffith and fined me $500.

Confident? After the Dodgers lost the first two games of the 1981 World Series to the Yankees, I ran into Mrs. Tom Bradley, wife of the mayor of Los Angeles, on a jet flight.

"I had a dream," I told her. "The Dodgers will win the next four." I also reminded her that the Dodgers had never had a ticker tape parade. And she said, "You take care of winning the World Series. I'll take care of the parade." I said, "You've got a deal."

One of my more memorable moments came in that

Series—the pinch home run off Ron Davis to help the Dodgers win game four, 8–7. There have been other highlights, of course—those productive years in Philly; the 10 for 22 streak with the Cubs in May 1983; watching Boston Red Sox manager Don Zimmer choke on his chewing tobacco when Bucky Dent homered off Mike Torres to win the 1978 AL East title for the Yankees.

But during the most thrilling moment of my baseball career, I simply stood and watched.

It was 1967, Yankee Stadium, New York. I was just a baby with the Angels, playing right field with my knees knocking. I'll never forget sneaking glances at those monuments in center field.

We won the first game of a doubleheader, and Mickey Mantle, the best switch-hitter I ever saw, had a tough time. He didn't even start game two, which we led, 2–1, going into the bottom of the ninth.

Now it's two out, runner on first base with a base on balls, and our manager, Bill Rigney, goes to the mound. He calls for relief pitcher Minnie Rojas. But as Minnie is warming up, the crowd starts roaring. Mantle has his foot on the top step of the dugout. The place is going bananas.

Now he walks to the plate, and when the PA announcer says, "Now batting, number seven, Mickey"—you can't hear him finish. The sound in that place was unbelievable, and I'm tingling.

Remember now, I'm in right field. I can see it just as clearly now as 18 years ago. Rojas throws a hellacious slider, and it was like a scene out of *The Natural.* One mighty swing—phoooohh—and I know I don't even have to move. I just stand there and watch as the ball soars high over my head to hit a girder at the top of the Yankee Stadium upper deck. If it doesn't hit that girder, it hits the subway.

Now there limps Mantle around the bases. He can hardly run, taped from his ankles to his thighs. And the noise was deafening. I'd never experienced anything like it and haven't since.

The Mantle home run stays with me. On the other hand, so does Frank Umont wiggling his hotfoot, Tom Lasorda screaming from his Dodgertown room, Jim Fregosi wondering (and knowing) who let the air out of his tires, Don Mincher bitching about his socks getting sewn together, and, oh, that look on Steve Garvey's face when he stuck his hand into a gooey brownie.

Did you know I once had lunch with USC football coach John McKay? Yessir, the quarterback from Edgewood High School, West Covina, California, had 35 football scholarship offers. I could run the 100-yard dash in 9.9 and even ran the anchor leg of the relay in my baseball spikes. I'd take off my baseball pants in the seventh inning and spring from the ball diamond to the track in shorts.

Sure, I played basketball too. Didn't all good athletes in high school? I liked all sports. But I loved baseball. My dad, John William, Sr., was an excellent athlete himself. He might have made it as a pro baseball player in the late 1930s, or maybe as an Olympic sprinter, if he hadn't gone into the military for World War II.

On the other hand, if he hadn't been diverted from Bataan to Australia during the Big War he wouldn't have met Audrey, my Aussie-born mother. She returned to Connecticut for my birth in 1946, and when I was in grade school we moved to California, where my dad continued in the dairy business.

He always pushed me to athletic excellence. And I have to chuckle inside when he always asks his half-Aussie son: "Why do they call you crazy?"

It sure beats me, Dad. I said it when I was a rookie, and I said it again this spring: I'm just glad to be here.

After all, timing is everything, isn't it? Like the time, 18 years ago, when I met my wife, Mary Jayne—who spelled it that way before Jayne Mansfield. We were both appearing at a boat show in Los Angeles. I was at a booth with Jim Fregosi pushing pearls. She was onstage smiling and charging people $5 to have their pictures taken with her.

During a break (Mary Jayne was an actress from age five, and probably appeared in several hundred movies and television shows), she wandered down to our booth (we were aspriring big-shot pearl importers), stuck her hand into a fish bowl, and came up with an oyster that had a pearl in it (okay, so maybe it was fixed).

Then, finding out we were ball players with the Angels, she invited us onstage to pose for a picture. I got stuck behind the blond (Mary Jayne), shoved my hands into the pocket of her jeans, lifted her into the air and said, "Gee, you're a short little shit, aren't you?"

Can you think of a more romantic introduction? We were married eleven months later because she insisted that if I wasn't serious, I should take a hike.

Mary Jayne gave up a successful career to be married to me, and I'm sure there have been times she's regretted it. At first, she took road trips that other wives wouldn't consider taking. She drove managers crazy. Whoever heard of a baseball wife going on the road with her husband in the 1960s? She even traveled with me in the minor leagues and still claims that the cockroaches in Hawaii have wings.

Nowadays she stays home in San Marino with Mary Jayne Sarah, born in 1980, and insists that if I ever get out of baseball, our marriage could be in deep trouble. She claims she counts the days until I go on the road and she can have peace of mind. Why do women say things like that?

Few baseball wives ever lived in as many places as Mary Jayne. To name a few: five locations in Florida, three in Arizona, three in Puerto Rico, Anaheim, Seattle, Chicago (twice), Los Angeles, Tucson, Oakland, Philadelphia, New Jersey, New York, Palm Springs (she didn't complain about that one), and Perrysburg, Ohio, where she was the number one bartender at the Ramada Inn.

She doesn't say things like "Jay got traded." She says, "*We* got traded."

I asked her the other day if she ever had second thoughts about marrying a ball player.

"No, she said, "but third, fourth, and fifth."

We were blessed beyond description when Mary Jayne Sarah was born after thirteen years of marriage. Has she had an impact on my life? Not much. I just can't keep my hands off her. And I think she likes me, too—at least when she sees me on television. Maybe that's where she learned, instead of calling me "Da-Da," to yell "Earth to Jay!" when she wants my attention.

Marriages change. Careers change. And certainly I'd be lying if I didn't say that the profession has changed. Mickey Vernon, now a hitting instructor with the Yankees, described perfectly just how *much* it has changed:

"We used to go to the racetrack after practice in my day," said Vernon. "Four of us would chip in 50 cents each at the $2 window."

"But the other day I asked a player how he did at the track, and he said, 'My horse won.' I said, 'How much did he pay?' and he said, 'No, coach, I didn't bet on the horse, I own it.' "

I don't own any horses—just some umbrella hats, some worn batting gloves, victory glasses, and a fond memory of my lost Star Patrol helmet.

And as long as this game is fun, and they'll have me, I plan to keep on playing. But if I look in the mirror and see a guy who's not having any fun, that's when I'll get out. And even then all my summers will be planned. I'll just go around playing in Old-Timers' games for all my ex-teams. My pal Jerry Reuss says that every game I play in is like an intrasquad game, anyhow.

How will I be remembered? Maybe someday a rookie will hear my name mentioned and say:

"Jay Johnstone? He was so crazy that when he came into the hotel room, his pillow jumped out the window."

And that kid might have a chance in this game.

ACKNOWLEDGMENTS

Sincere thanks to all who shared the experiences and anecdotes that appear in this book. And to anybody else who has gotten a good belly laugh from baseball—from ball players, managers, coaches, trainers, and team doctors to umpires, traveling secretaries, sportswriters, announcers, groundskeepers, scoreboard operators, vendors, security guards—and especially to the fans of this little boys' game—just a piece of advice: keep smiling. It often makes the losing easier and has even been known to win a game or two.

Also, special thanks to special friends: Tommy Lasorda, whose faith in me has kept me going and who has been like a father to me; Bob Saunders, my father-in-law, a man who taught me to grow up to *be* a man; Crazy Larry McTague and Dr. Archie, who showed me life in New York's fast lane and how to cope with it; Mike De Stefano, the South Philadelphia Eighth Street genius, who handled my PR during my five years in Philly; Cy Sussman of the William Morris Agency; Arthur Adler of Adler Communications in New York; Mike Corey of PACE; Mike Roarty and Charlie Head at Budweiser in St. Louis; Charlie Olson of Chicago's Ultimate Sports Bar and Grill, who kept me out of trouble when I could have been out carousing; Joey Mondelli of Kelly Mondelli's restaurant in Chicago, who fed me nightly and kept my spirits up; Ken Wells, my high school coach, who helped put my career on the right track; Gus DeJohn of WSNI radio and Ron Lovelace in Philadelphia, who have remained my friends throughout my career, through the good times and the bad; and Shari Lesser, my editor, who someday will be a great major league manager.

Finally, to all the men like my father, who gave up dreams of being athletes to fight in wars and defend their country so that their families could grow up free in the greatest nation in the world, and to my many friends who lost their lives fighting in Vietnam: all the respect, admiration, and gratitude I can offer.